YOUR INNER GOLF GURU

DEVELOPING THE GOLF INSTRUCTOR WITHIN

James Ragonnet, Ph.D.

SPORTS PUBLISHING

Sports Publishing books may be purchased in bulk at special discounts for sales promotion, corporate gifts, fund-raising, or educational purposes. Special editions can also be created to specifications. For details, contact the Special Sales Department, Sports Publishing, 307 West 36th Street, 11th Floor, New York, NY 10018 or info@skyhorsepublishing.com.

Sports Publishing® is a registered trademark of Skyhorse Publishing, Inc.®, a Delaware corporation.

Visit our website at www.skyhorsepublishing.com.

10 9 8 7 6 5 4 3 2 1

Library of Congress Cataloging-in-Publication Data is available on file.

Cover design by Mona Lin
Cover photo by Getty Images

ISBN: 978-1-68358-398-1
Ebook ISBN: 978-1-68358-399-8

Printed in the United States of America

Contents

Introduction   vii

Thinking about Thinking   1

Systems Theory   7

White Matter   11

Mastering Complex Skills   15

Spraying and Praying   19

The Three Stages   21

Engrams   25

Educated Hands   29

Focus   39

Structure   43

Ball Flight Laws   49

Rocking and Throwing   53

Consistency and Variability   61

Mirror Neurons   65

Learned Helplessness   71

Unlearning   73

Robin Hood   81

Choking under Pressure   85

Weighted Clubs   93
Golfers and Dieters   97
Models   101
Paul Runyan   109
Confirmation Bias   115
The Mind's Eye   119
A Yardstick for Failure   123
Why You Have a Brain   125
Breathing   129
Intellect vs. Intelligence   133
Great Expectations   137
Neurogenesis   141
Instant Gratification   145
Rx Golf   149
Autodidacts   155
Clutter   159
Cognitive Dissonance   163
No Sacred Cows   169
Bamboozled   173
Big Data   177
Observational Learning   183
The Grass Whip   187
Smarts   193
The Transition   197
Practice   201
Eye Tracking   209
Sherlock Holmes   215
Arcs and Straight Lines   219

Rebellious Discernment   227

Optical Illusions   233

The Follow-through   239

Less Is More   243

Fleeting Indicators   249

References   253

Introduction

*"You will have to create the path by walking yourself;
the path is not ready-made, lying there and waiting for you."*
— Osho

When I was a teenager, I painstakingly studied Ben Hogan's *Power Golf* and *The Five Lessons: The Modern Fundamentals of Golf*. However, Hogan's teachings about binding one's arms together, winding up one's core muscles, centering one's weight over the front leg in the backswing, and imagining the swing plane as a pane of glass didn't make sense to me. What made sense to Hogan didn't make sense to me.

Hogan's teachings, I later realized, were actually based on feelings—not factual and scientific evidence. Hogan wasn't doing what he said he was doing. Hogan's teachings were mostly ineffectual. To swing like Hogan, I needed his inquisitiveness, intellect, flexibility, strength, talent, personality, experience, coordination, determination, balance, work ethic, and central nervous system.

For decades, I searched for the optimal guru whose foolproof methodology promoted rapid improvement among all golfers. However, I never found one. Underwriters Laboratory Inc. doesn't test and certify golf methodologies. Moreover, the PGA, USGA, and National Golf Foundation do not track the improvement rates of pupils and the teaching success of certified instructors.

Admittedly, I've encountered many excellent and diverse instructors who've developed excellent players. However, I've never encountered a single instructor who was completely accurate and universally effective.

Most golf experts are essentially ball-striking instructors. To lower one's score, instructors teach swing mechanics. Herein lies the problem. Most instructors, including the most talented and respected, base their teaching and learning on a narrow scientific platform.

Today's instructors—assisted by computer diagnostics—teach ball striking dictated primarily by physics, biomechanics, and kinesiology. There's nothing wrong with that. However, this limited platform ignores a host of applicable sciences, including geometry, anatomy, cognitive psychology, neuroscience, neurobiology, statistics, game theory, systems theory, learning theory, heuristics, etc.

The swing is a holistic, dynamic, and complex movement. Therefore, what may be optimal from a biomechanical standpoint may not be from a neuroscientific or anatomical standpoint and vice versa. Moreover, certain golfers will connect better with the principles of one particular science and not another. The ultimate guru must understand and apply *all* the underlying sciences associated with ball striking to golfers of every skill level, learning style, and cognitive ability—from novices to Tour pros. I question whether the ultimate guru actually exists.

After decades of endless struggle and marginal improvement, I stopped expecting surrogates to actualize my growth. I stopped assuming that only gurus bearing gifts could enhance my game.

When I put stock in self-knowledge, self-teaching, and self-scrutiny, I resolved to customize, individualize, hybridize, personalize, and freelance my own methodology. If you don't evolve your own methodology, you'll be enslaved by someone else's.

A *guru* is a Hindu teacher, mentor, guide, expert, or master who actualizes the potentialities of others. In Sanskrit, *gu* means darkness and *ru* means destroyer. Gurus are literally destroyers of darkness and ignorance. Relying on a golf guru is like employing a raft to cross a hazardous river. Once you cross the river, you must leave the raft behind. Dragging along the raft will slow down your journey. When you need to cross the next river, another raft awaits.

When I became my own guru, I started to recognize blind spots, sift through advice, defy convention, revolutionize my thinking, reverse my instincts, discover new insights, expand my imagination, test different approaches, connect the dots, and experience moments of supreme lucidity. Most important, I began to understand what works, what doesn't, and why.

In the process of becoming my own guru, I no longer placed others on a pedestal, expected others to make me whole, or subordinated my thinking to suit others. Don't get me wrong. I still seek outside advice. I still drink from as many wells as possible. However, I no longer grant others dominion over me. I destroy my own darkness and ignorance.

Only I can walk in my shoes . . . only I can experience my uncertainties, frustrations, and disappointments . . . only I can achieve my dreams and aspirations . . . only I can define my golf reality . . . only I can actualize growth . . . only I can self-learn.

Becoming your own guru entails risk. However, turning your game over to someone else and hoping for the best entail greater risk. T.S. Eliot wrote, "Only those who will risk going too far can possibly find out how far one can go." You—not someone else—are the most powerful determinant of who you are.

When I vowed to become my own golf guru, I examined the findings of enlightened thinkers. This book—an oasis for worn and weary golfers—is a repository of these findings. "I do not teach anyone," Einstein wrote, "I only provide an environment in which they can learn." *Learning how to learn* and *learning how to motivate yourself to learn* are life's most important endeavors.

I can't predict whether you'll become your own golf guru. But I can predict that taking responsibility for yourself will bring you immense satisfaction. If you're willing to spend the time and energy to improve, you might as well enjoy it.

When I embarked on my path of self-discovery, my inner guru emerged. Accordingly, I spawned a radical approach to learning the golf swing that merges the untapped and unlikely domains of cognitive neuroscience *and* systemic thinking. Once these applications took root, I dramatically improved my game. I still seek out gifted and diverse teachers—not to tell me what to do, but to guide my inner guru. Let me explain.

Cognitive Neuroscience.

The *mind* is a nonphysical faculty that encompasses consciousness, imagination, perception, thinking, judgment, language, and memory. The soft science of the mind is called "cognitive psychology."

The *brain* is a physical organ whose 86 billion neurons communicate by employing trillions of connections. The hard science of the brain is called "neuroscience." The science that merges *mind* and *brain* is called "cognitive neuroscience."

Understanding how your mind, brain, and muscles function enables you to process information, make decisions, build and reinforce neural pathways, induce muscle contractions, store memories, adapt to changing conditions, sharpen thinking, enhance learning, identify bad habits, minimize breakdowns, and induce growth. When you finally integrate mind, brain, and body, your counterintuitive and puzzling swing will start to make sense.

Your brain's neocortex is hard-wired to seek certainty. Golfers addicted to certainty often embrace the unexamined and unchallenged beliefs of self-confident experts. When you integrate mind and brain, you'll mitigate your craving for certainty. Dr. Robert Burton, Chief of Neurology at the University of California, said, "We need to recognize that the feelings of certainty and conviction are involuntary mental sensations—not logical conclusions." Illusions of certainty stunt growth.

Noted psychologist Erick Fromm wrote, "The quest for certainty blocks the search for meaning. Uncertainty is the very condition that impels us to unfold our powers." Remain open-minded.

Your thoughts and feelings affect how your mind, brain, and body function. Your mind and brain are constantly interpreting a wealth of sensory input, body movements, and emotional states. Focusing your attention and sharpening your awareness let you understand the internal workings of your mind, brain, and muscles. The lessons in this book are designed to *name* and *tame* the ingrained behaviors and faulty reasoning that sabotage your performance.

In a nutshell, you must change your thinking... to change your learning . . . to change your movement patterns. The proper integration of mind, brain, and body will induce deep learning. Objective introspection—the prerequisite for growth—will temper your emotional impulses and allow your native intelligence or inner guru to emerge. Leo Rosten wrote, "We see things as *we* are, not as *they* are." Your main golf problem isn't your swing. Rather, it's your distorted perception of what you're thinking, learning, and doing.

If you're not improving, you're a prisoner of your brain's 86 billion hard-wired neurons that plan, coordinate, and control your movements. Bad habits reinforced over time—such as fast tempos, loopy swings, and incorrect grips—are hard to break. The interlocking processes of *learning, unlearning,* and *relearning* demand mental exertion, tireless motivation, and deliberate practice.

However, old dogs *can* learn new tricks. The term *neuroplasticity* denotes the brain's ability under proper conditions to change its structure and function over your lifetime. This is reassuring news for stymied golfers.

You rewire your brain by adding *myelin* or insulating layers of fatty tissue to the lengthy fibers that transmit electrical impulses to your brain cells. The myelination process increases the speed and frequency of the impulses that induce muscle contractions and movement patterns. "Deliberate practice"—the ceaseless process of repeating selected movements, self-monitoring your performance, and remediating mistakes—thickens the myelin layers of your neural pathways. Deliberate practice converts meandering neural trickles into flowing neural streams.

Neural circuits are like growth rings in a tree trunk. New neural circuits overwrite, but don't eradicate, existing ones. To initiate swing changes and generate new neural pathways, you need approximately one hundred slow-motion repetitions. To make a default or long-term swing change, you'll need hundreds of repetitions. It's imperative, therefore, that every swing change be spot-on. Every mile you travel in the wrong direction, by ingraining incorrect movement patterns, is a two-mile mistake.

Bad habits are hard to break. In sum, you must *unlearn* before you can *relearn*. Young golfers with thinly insulated neural pathways improve more rapidly than older golfers. To rid their bad habits, older golfers need tremendous willpower or mental bandwidth. It's easier to uproot a sapling than a giant oak.

Systemic Thinking.

Systems theory, proposed in the 1950s and popularized in the 1970s, denotes the interdisciplinary study of mechanical and social networks comprised of interrelated and interdependent parts.

Systemic thinking is a way of viewing and understanding how interdependent parts in a network interact to achieve a unified and specific purpose.

Systemic thinking fosters understanding by examining the connections among its parts—not by examining its parts taken separately. Systemic thinking, which *unites* components, focuses on the whole. Analytical thinking, which *separates* components, focuses on the parts.

To better understand and manage your swing, you must merge analytical and systemic thinking. Some problems are best solved analytically. Others are best solved systemically.

However, systemic thinking has been grossly overlooked in golf instruction. To understand and manage your swing, a complex and holistic movement involving a myriad of interdependent parts, you must invoke systemic thinking.

Albert Einstein famously said, "We cannot solve our problems with the same thinking we used to create them." Most people will agree with Einstein's statement. However, very few people, especially golfers, understand what it means. It means that golfers cannot solve their swing problems by using the analytical mode of thinking that created them in the first place.

Analysis, the process of taking things apart, seems like the obvious way to foster understanding. For decades I tried to understand and improve my swing by employing analytical thinking. However, I was wrong. Taking apart my swing often made it worse. When you disassemble a whole, it loses its essential properties, and so do all of its parts.

To understand my swing as a holistic motion, I had to view it systemically. I had to understand the interactions among its many parts.

In *The Effective Executive* (1967), Peter Drucker makes a key distinction between *doing the thing right* and *doing the right thing*. For example, Japanese car makers are *doing the thing right* by mass-producing inexpensive and fuel-efficient vehicles. However, they're not *doing the right thing, as* Japanese cars have greatly exacerbated global warming. Peter Drucker said, "There's nothing worse than doing the wrong thing well."

Drucker's statement aptly conveys what's wrong with modern golf instruction. *Taking apart the swing analytically destroys its holistic nature.*

Golfers who analyze the swing by dividing it into separate parts are *doing things right.* However, golfers who synthesize the swing by aggregating the parts are *doing the right thing. Doing the thing right* is the mark of efficiency. *Doing the right thing* is the mark of wisdom.

You can't repair a highly complex system by improving each part taken separately. To repair a highly complex system, you must improve the simultaneous interactions among all its parts. A system is not the sum of its parts, but the product of their interactions.

Suppose you installed a Rolls Royce motor, BMW transmission, Audi fuel pump, and Cadillac disc brakes in your Hyundai to improve its performance. What would happen? Your Hyundai wouldn't function. Why? Because these parts don't fit. Suppose you installed Hogan's backswing, Snead's footwork, Nicklaus's release, and Faldo's pivot to improve your golf swing. What would happen? Your swing wouldn't function. Why? Because these parts don't fit.

Your swing components must fit your unique parameters. Your golf swing—like your fingerprint or signature—is uniquely yours. Swing components that work for someone else may not work for you.

The golf swing lasts only 1.4 seconds; incorporates hidden forces and pressures; involves 206 bones, 360 joints, and 600 muscles; and contains a myriad of interactions. A systems approach is the only way to understand and master the swing. Analytical approaches alone don't work.

Understanding how a component functions in a system is meaningless unless you understand how it interacts directly or indirectly with every other component. In the swing's tightly coupled system, everything depends on everything else. No component functions in isolation.

Small movements that most golfers dismiss offhandedly—such as lifting your heel, turning your chin, softening your lead arm, bending your knees, and hinging your wrists—are profoundly important. Adopting a system's perspective helps you identify and understand the intricate interrelationship among your swing's many components.

Using analytical or anti-systemic thinking to teach and learn the swing is pointless. Given the swing's tightly coupled system, understanding how any separate component *acts*—such as the hands, wrists, arms, or shoulders—is irrelevant unless you understand how this component *interacts* directly or indirectly with every other component. Golf's accepted "divide and conquer" mode of teaching and learning—invoked in most instructional protocols—doesn't work.

In his article, "Golf Swing Mechanics: The Path to the Future Golf Swing," physicist Dr. René Ferdinand states, ". . . it only takes one incorrect piece of information to make a whole golf swing system invalid or difficult to perform."

Tightly coupled, complex systems break down when small glitches converge in unexpected and hidden ways. In tightly coupled, complex systems, there's very little slack, clearance, or margin of error.

A *simple* system—like a rudimentary assembly line in a cookie factory comprised of *loosely* coupled components—experiences breakdowns that are relatively easy to spot, diagnose, and repair. Conversely, a *complex* system, like a nuclear reactor aboard a submarine, is prone to breakdowns that are very difficult to spot, diagnose, and repair.

Selected components in your tightly coupled swing—such as your grip and stance—have sufficient slack or tolerance, whereas other swing components—such as your pivot and club face angle at impact—have less slack or tolerance.

The swing is far more complex, paradoxical, and illusory than most suppose. Adopting a systems approach will suspend your fuzzy thinking, default reasoning, erroneous assumptions, snap judgments, screwy biases, simplistic solutions, and quick fixes. Sports psychologists claim that golf's physical and mental skill sets, except for those of pole vaulting, are the hardest to master.

My eclectic scientific platform, bolstered by decades of playing, coaching, teaching, researching, and writing, originated during my doctoral studies at Rensselaer Polytechnic Institute. When I completed my dissertation, which examined the cognitive strategies of brilliant, imaginative, and iconoclastic scientists, I experienced a paradigm shift. I developed a Veggie Chopper brain and changed my thinking.

This book is a logical extension of my previous book, *Golf's Three Noble Truths: The Fine Art of Playing Awake*, acknowledged by PGA coaches including those affiliated with Justin Rose, Phil Mickelson, Jim Furyk, Steve Elkington, and D.J. Trahan.

This book's brief, reader-friendly, and research-based lessons encourage golfers to take responsibility for what they think and why they think it. Assembled here is the advice of players and diverse experts from the realms of coaching, biomechanics, physics, anatomy, genetics, kinesiology, learning theory, cognitive psychology, neuroscience, neurobiology, systems theory, behavioral psychology, educational psychology, management theory, game theory, sociology, economics, etc. Each self-contained lesson aims to hone your thinking, learning, and performing.

The juxtaposition of these lessons is deliberate. Education specialists claim that "juxtaposed learning"—the presentation of disparate ideas from multiple disciplines—cultivates engagement, creativity, and understanding. Juxtaposed learning infused with humor reportedly induces imaginative leaps, sharper focus, creative insights, bold connections, and rapid learning.

The term *disruptive innovation* denotes the introduction of a new, radical, and efficient development that takes root, becomes more accessible, displaces an established mechanism, and induces rapid change. Applying *cognitive neuroscience* and *systemic thinking* to master the golf swing is a disruptive innovation whose time has come. Science fiction writer William Gibson wrote, "The future is already here—it's just not evenly distributed."

In bookstores and libraries, the shelves containing books on cognitive science and systems theory AND those containing books on golf and self-help are widely separated. My book straddles this gap.

Your ability to outthink, outlearn and outperform your opponents is your greatest advantage. The best time to realize that advantage was years ago. The second-best time is now.

Thinking about
Thinking

That large trash barrel jam-packed with discarded drivers, fairway woods, hybrids, chippers, putters, wedges, and assorted training aids in your garage is a repository of snap decisions, impulsive judgments, reckless spending, distorted logic, false assumptions, inaccurate information, grand illusions, gut reactions, careless observations, quick fixes, and blind faith.

Natural selection over thousands of years has equipped humans for survival with fast thinking, gut reactions, and intuitive responses. However, fast thinking is unsuitable for making sound decisions, solving intricate problems, and mastering complex skills.

Fast thinking provides you with enough information to believe you're right, but insufficient knowledge to know you're wrong.

In his book *Thinking, Fast and Slow* (2013), cognitive psychologist Daniel Kahneman identifies two types of thinking: "System 1 or fast thinking operates automatically and quickly with little or no effort and no sense of voluntary control. System 2 or slow thinking allocates attention to the effortful mental activities that demand it, including complex computations."

Slow thinking is demanding and exhausting. Your brain, which consumes 20 percent of your energy intake, operates mostly on low-energy fast thinking. Failed golfers addicted to low-energy fast thinking seek quick fixes and simplistic solutions.

Suppose your major swing problem is *coming over the top*. You want to eliminate—not fix—this problem. Eliminating a swing problem demands deep understanding and high-energy thinking. Fixing a swing problem demands superficial understanding and low-energy thinking.

Fast and slow thinking are situational. Admittedly, fast thinking—guided by hunches, emotions, and quick recall—often yields sound decisions and positive results. If you want to add 8 and 21, for example, fast thinking works. However, if you want to multiply 8 x 28, fast thinking doesn't work.

If fast thinking works well most of the time, then what's the problem? The problem is *compatibility*. If your unconscious, low-energy, fast thinking is your default mode, you'll never know how and when to engage conscious, high-energy, slow thinking.

It's not enough to know *how* and *what* you're thinking. You need to know *why* you're thinking it. If you don't monitor your thoughts, you'll jump to conclusions, become over-confident, reject opposing views, entertain biases, and take mental short-cuts. According to Søren Kierkegaard, people are fooled in two ways: they believe what isn't true and they reject what is true.

When it comes to maximizing your performance, ignore what the majority thinks and does. When individuals hit a wall or an impasse, according to researchers, they do one of two things: (1) they do more of the same or (2) they do less of the same. Only 3 percent do something new or different. The remaining 97 percent continue to smash against the wall by doing the same thing in varying degrees.

When brain scientists are asked, "What is the purpose of thinking?" they often respond sarcastically by saying: "The purpose of thinking is to *stop thinking*." Since thinking is a high-energy activity, people prefer default thinking or auto-pilot thinking. However, auto-pilot thinking is precarious.

If you consider yourself a cogent thinker, think again. According to cognitive scientists Hugo Mercier and Dan Sperber—authors of *The Enigma of Reason* (2017)—humans systematically make decisions that defy clear logic. They write, "The main role of reasoning in decision-making is not to arrive at the decision but to be able to present the decision as something that's rational."

For example, if you decide to change your stance or posture based on fast thinking, you'll retrospectively engage slow thinking to justify your decision. Mercier and Sperber use the term "myside bias" to denote the tendency to spot the flawed thinking and ignore your own. That's why you can spot flaws in others, but not in yourself.

To think about thinking, nourish your awareness. You can't change anything that escapes your awareness. Moreover, you can't expect others to sharpen your thinking. Others can create a context for sharpening your thinking. However, rational thinking is a gift you must give to yourself. To change your thinking, you must recognize your *explicit* and *implicit* biases.

Explicit or conscious biases—like your decided preference for TaylorMade drivers and Mizuno irons—are easy to recognize. However, *implicit* biases, like your slumped posture or weak grip, are more insidious. Implicit biases allow you to process vast amounts of complex information; however, they're difficult to recognize.

Kahneman's book, which abounds with examples of implicit and unconscious biases, cites a research study by Shai Danzinger, who examined the results of 1,112 Israeli parole hearings. Danzinger found that judges tended to deny paroles just before lunch to expedite slow and lengthy hearings.

Danzinger writes, "The judges' behavior can be easily explained. All repetitive decision-making tasks drain our mental resources. We start suffering from *choice overload* and we start opting for the easiest choice." Judges, mentally drained from listening to a succession of lengthy hearings, employ default fast thinking to deny parole requests. Taking a break will restore your slow thinking.

Experienced and intelligent people—including judges, physicians, engineers, and golfers—unwittingly make bad decisions based on implicit biases and low-energy thinking. If you're at the mercy of cognitive forces you can't perceive or control, you're going to make some colossal mistakes. To improve your game, examine *what* you're thinking and *why*.

The *availability heuristic* is a mental shortcut employed by most fast-thinking golfers. Kahneman writes, "The technical definition of *heuristic* is a simple procedure that helps find adequate, though imperfect, answers to difficult questions. The word comes from the same root as *eureka* [to discover]."

The availability heuristic employs trial-and-error reasoning, stereotyping, common sense, intuition, educated guesses, and other approaches to solve problems and make decisions. Golfers routinely make bad decisions based on the availability heuristic. When you solve problems and make decisions, your lazy brain tends to retrieve the most recent information first—not the most relevant and accurate information. Most golfers believe *the latest is the greatest*.

Golfers often make decisions and solve problems based on new information gleaned from websites, television, magazines, books, instructors, and mentors. The availability heuristic explains why every new solution is often another new mistake. Most golfers who immediately latch onto the latest guru, driver, or swing theory suffer from what psychologists call FOMO—*the fear of missing out*.

To test his availability heuristic hypothesis, Kahneman asked subjects to list words beginning with *K* (e.g., kitchen, kangaroo, kale) and words whose third letter is *K* (e.g., baker, acknowledge, fake). Kahneman's subjects found more words beginning with a *K* even though there are three times as many English words with *K* in third position.

It takes more mental effort to think of words with *K* in third position. According to Kahneman, people make snap decisions based on shallow, low-energy fast thinking—not on deep, high-energy slow thinking. Fast thinking is your brain's default mode. However, there are exceptions.

Your brain will automatically extinguish biases and engage high-energy slow thinking in the face of imminent failure during high-stakes competition. In their article "Is Tiger Woods Loss Averse?" economists Devin Pope and Maurice Schweitzer discuss the issue of *loss aversion* in relation to fast and slow thinking.

Loss aversion involves weighing two competing motives: *avoiding losses* vs. *achieving gains*. Avoiding losses, the more powerful motive, automatically engenders high-energy slow thinking. In other words, you'll concentrate more when you're putting to avoid a bogie than when you're putting to make a birdie.

Pope and Schweitzer, who studied 2.5 million PGA putts, reasoned that Tour pros concentrate more intensely when putting to save pars than to make birdies. According to their study, Tour pros made 3.6 percent more par putts than birdie putts of comparable length. (This small percentage of par putts represented over $1 million in Tiger's annual earnings.) It's not that you'll deliberately slack off when putting for birdie. It's that your cognitive intensity increases when you're trying to avoid losses. Too much or too little cognitive intensity is detrimental. Therefore, balance fast and slow thinking accordingly.

Kahneman's main thesis is noteworthy: people make snap decisions and jump to conclusions based on biases and false information. He uses the acronym *WYSIATI*, meaning *"What you see is all there is."* This notion relates directly to improving your swing. If you have a WYSIATI mindset, you'll identify *obvious* factors and ignore *hidden* factors.

The golf swing—a highly complex, dynamic, and nuanced athletic motion of brief duration—contains a myriad of invisible and illusionary pressures, forces, and movements. Actually, it's easier to learn how to pitch a baseball—an athletic motion comprised of a windup, delivery, and follow-through lasting 2.5 seconds—than to learn how to hit a golf ball.

An unchecked WYSIATI mindset—incompatible with understanding and mastering complex movements—invites casual observation, erroneous assumptions, fast thinking, and snap judgments. Simply stated, the golf swing is far more intricate and elusive than you suppose. To learn and understand the swing, you must look deeply, ask questions, think slowly, and become objectively introspective.

When you think about thinking, your learning habits will improve dramatically. Acquiring new skills gets easier when you pay attention to *what* you're thinking and *why* you're thinking it. Careless thinking arises quickly. Critical thinking arises slowly. Despite the brain's awesome capacity, humans think poorly. Learning *how* to think is more important than learning *what* to think.

Sigmund Freud claimed that our native intelligence emerges ". . . only when it is removed from the influence of strong emotion." To think efficiently, you need *objective introspection.*

Systems Theory

During the Congressional hearings investigating The Challenger Space Shuttle disaster in 1986, Richard Feynman, a Nobel Laureate physicist at Caltech, conducted a miniexperiment. Feynman dropped a rubber O-ring in a glass of ice water to simulate the freezing temperatures prior to the launch. After ten seconds, the rubber O-ring, comparable to the large rubber gaskets on the rocket boosters, became rigid and snapped. To explain the horrific explosion of the spacecraft, Feynman said, "I believe this has some significance for our problem."

Feynman, who viewed the space shuttle as a tightly coupled network of innumerable, interdependent components, invoked systems thinking to solve a complex problem. A brilliant thinker, Feynman traced the cause of The Challenger disaster to a seemingly insignificant O-ring.

A space shuttle, large corporation, nuclear reactor, human body, and golf swing are systems. A *system* is defined as an indivisible whole consisting of two or more components. No component in a system exists in isolation. The golf swing is a *complex system.*

There are two kinds of systems: *linear* and *complex.* A linear system—like an assembly line in a cookie factory—is relatively easy to understand. A complex system—like a nuclear

7

reactor—is hard to understand. Linear systems are straightforward. Complex systems are chaotic. Swinging a golf club is essentially an exercise in chaos control.

Sociologist Charles Perrow classifies complex systems as *loosely coupled* or *tightly coupled*. Components in a loosely coupled system are slower, weaker, less essential, and more observable, whereas components in tightly coupled systems are faster, stronger, more essential, and less observable. Glitches in tightly coupled components induce cascading failures. The golf swing—like any complex system—is inherently failure prone.

Would you expect Homer Simpson, who lacks a fundamental understanding of complex systems, to manage a nuclear reactor? Similarly, would you expect golfers who lack a fundamental understanding of complex systems to manage their golf swings? Nuclear reactors and golf swings—both complex, tightly coupled systems—are problematic.

In his book *The Fifth System*, management expert Peter Senge wrote, "Systems thinking is a discipline for seeing wholes. It is a framework for seeing inter-relationships rather than things, for seeing patterns of change rather than static snapshots . . . Today, systems thinking is needed more than ever because we are becoming overwhelmed by complexity."

Systems thinking will help you understand and remedy your complex golf swing. Applying systems thinking to the swing or any complex network containing many interrelated parts is a daunting task. That's why so few people do it.

In his article "A Lifetime of Systems Thinking," Russell Ackoff makes two key assertions that relates to all golfers: (1) *To improve a system, you must understand the interactions among its components and (2) All systems are multidisciplinary.*

Installing a pivot or backswing taken from someone else's swing system won't necessarily improve your swing. Installing a kidney or liver taken from someone else's anatomical system won't necessarily improve your health. Instructors ignorant of the swing's multidisciplinary and systemic nature are peddling fake panaceas.

To fathom complex relationships, process sensory feedback, and effect significant swing changes, think systemically.

Tom Watson, who understood the daunting challenge of merging analytical thinking and systemic thinking, said, "To me, a great golfer illustrates two very precise pictures. One is proper fundamentals. The other is unencumbered motion. Without the first, it follows that the second is impossible to produce."

Viewing the swing as a complex system helps you understand how the bigger and slower muscles in your trunk and lower body govern the faster muscles in your arms and hands. Therefore, place the center of gravity in your swing as low as possible such as on your pelvis.

The *static* elements in your swing (i.e., your grip, stance, bracing your trailing knee, alignment, posture) can be easily monitored and consciously controlled. The *dynamic* elements in your swing (i.e., your backswing, swing plane, pivot, hand path, kinetic sequence, lag angle) rely on sensory feedback with the exception of the "moment of truth." Impact, which happens automatically in 1/1,200th of a second, demands ingrained kinesthetic responses, not conscious controls.

Despite your illusions, your brain is not hardwired to send instantaneous and conscious commands to your bones, muscles, and joints. To swing autonomously, subconsciously, and kinesthetically requires deliberate practice.

All systems and subsystems are interdisciplinary. Therefore, creative solutions often reside outside your existing system.

When senior mechanical engineers spent months studying ways to speed up elevators in high-rise office buildings, a young engineer solved the problem simply by reframing the problem. He suggested that the problem with slow elevators was *behavioral,* not *mechanical.* In sum, the people waiting for the elevator were bored. To solve the boredom issue, he proposed installing mirrors in the boarding areas so people can occupy themselves by gawking inconspicuously at members of the opposite sex and admiring themselves.

Your swing problem is *cognitive,* not *biomechanical.*

White Matter

When you arrive at the course, you enter the locker room to change into your golf shoes. As you're tying your shoelaces, you make small talk with your playing partner. You don't have to think about tying your shoes. You do it automatically.

Do you remember when you learned to tie your shoelaces? It took several days to learn it. You had to decide which lace to tie first. You had to establish postural stability by bracing your back against a wall. You had to ensure that both laces were equal in length. You had to coordinate the movements of both hands. You had to employ approximately 138 muscles in your fingers, thumbs, hands, palms, and forearms and exert the precise amount of pressure.

You used one hand to hold the lace and the other to form the loop. You had to focus intently to connect the loops. Then you had to practice. Originally, tying your shoelaces was hard. Now it's easy.

When you learn a new skill, you change the deep wiring in your brain. Your brain's "gray matter" is composed of neurons that communicate through synapses. "Gray matter"—your brain's topsoil—is responsible for neural computation and information processing.

Beneath the gray matter is the "white matter" that fills nearly 50 percent of your brain. Your "white matter"—composed of bundled axons—contain fibers that carry electrical impulses that jump between neurons. Your deep brain or "white matter" is composed of white, fatty tissue or *myelin* that wraps around the axons. White matter is the tissue through which messages flow between different areas of gray matter in your central nervous system.

In his book *The Talent Code* (2009), Daniel Coyle describes myelin as "a dense fat that wraps itself like electrical tape around a nerve fiber, preventing the electrical impulses from leaking out." Myelination, the process of layering fatty tissue on nerve fibers, increases the speed and strength of electrical impulses that jump across neurons. Repeated practice thickens myelin layers.

Let's examine how nerve signals work. Your brain has approximately 86 billion *neurons* or building blocks. *Dendrites*—long and thin filaments attached to neurons—receive signals from other neurons. The tiny gaps between the dendrites are called *synapses*. Between the neuron and dendrites are *axons*—resembling cables—that transmit signals to other neurons. Dendrites receive signals. Axons send signals.

When different parts of your brain communicate and coordinate with one another, axons coated with *myelin* send electrical charges to other neurons. Firing electrically charged neurons resemble a falling stack of dominoes. A single dendrite can make as many as 10,000 connections.

In his article "The Other Half of the Brain," Douglas Fields states that nerve impulses race down axons 100 times faster when they are coated with myelin and that certain segments of axons are wrapped with as many as 150 separate myelin layers. When axons are heavily wrapped with myelin, electrical impulses can jump more swiftly from neuron to neuron. When axons are poorly wrapped with myelin, signals leak and dissipate.

Males have more plentiful and longer myelinated axons than females. Males at age 20 have approximately 105 miles of myelin compared to 92 miles for females. After age 20—as your axons diminish—your myelin levels decrease about 10 percent per decade.

To determine the role that myelin plays in the acquisition of complex skills, neuroscientists experimented on mice. The mice in Group One were trained to run on a wheel with some missing rungs. The mice in Group Two—the control group—were trained to run on a normal running wheel.

Initially, Group One mice stumbled over the missing rungs. With practice, however, they learned to anticipate the missing rungs and step over them. Eventually, they learned to run on the wheel with ease. Examining the brains of mice, neuroscientists concluded that mice need *new* myelin to learn new tasks and perform efficiently. Regardless of the synaptic changes in their gray matter, the mice needed to recruit new white matter—or myelin—to master the running wheel.

To learn new skills efficiently, golfers need to produce new "white matter" or myelin to speed the transmission of impulses through neural circuits. Neuroscientists insist that the brain keeps producing myelin as you age provided you practice selected skills frequently and correctly.

Focused and deliberate practice optimizes the production of myelin. As children absorb new information, they produce rich amounts of myelin. As adults absorb new information, they produce myelin more slowly and in smaller amounts. To learn new skills, aging golfers must expend considerable effort.

Since practice produces myelin, you must learn *what* and *how* to practice. If you repeatedly practice the wrong takeaway, for example, you'll myelinate axons that reinforce bad habits that are hard to correct. Therefore, learn and practice correct movement patterns. Hardwiring the wrong movement patterns will retard your growth.

Myelin regulates the speed of nerve impulses. Your myelin layers thicken every time you perform a motor skill. That's why skills—like tying your shoes—get easier with repetition.

Myelination is largely finished by the time you're twenty-five. However, that doesn't mean that you can't learn, unlearn, and relearn new skills later in life. Some researchers suggest that myelination continues until your midfifties, but at a slower rate. To learn new and complex skills, practice deliberately to recruit white matter. As recently as fifteen years ago, neuroscientists regarded white matter—compared to gray matter—as a passive and subordinate tissue. No more! From a learning perspective, "white matter" matters more.

Mastering
Complex Skills

At the Whiskey River Saloon in Whitefish, Montana, with several of your smug nongolfer buddies present, you want to demonstrate that hitting a golf ball is a daunting task. Each golf swing, regardless of how many times you practice it, is always slightly different from the previous one. Your brain plans every swing anew and slightly differently.

You tell your buddies that the human brain—subjected to a range of variables, conditions, and criteria—initiates a new and specific motor response for every complex movement. In sum, your neurons trigger a new and different sequencing pattern for your body's 600 muscles every time you swing.

Before you demonstrate the complexity of arranging a precise collision between the pea-size, sweet spot on a golf ball and the pea-size, sweet spot on an angled steel blade attached to a flexible 38" graphite shaft in a fluid downswing lasting only .4 seconds, you explain that mental and muscular tension further complicates things.

Now you're ready. Gripping a five-iron in your right hand, you mount the mechanical bull in the center of the dance floor. (Some rodeo bars charge $10 for a two-minute ride; however, the mechanical bull at the Whiskey River Saloon is free.)

You take a final glance at the golf ball on the ground, then push the red button on the pommel.

Akin to the forces in the golf swing, but far more wrenching, your body's 600 muscles, 206 bones, and 360 joints start moving up and down, side to side, and around and around. After you gain a modicum of composure, you prepare to swing. Grasping the pommel firmly with your left hand and gripping your five-iron in your right, you swing the club. Unfortunately, you make weak contact. You hit the ball in the direction of the service bar and watch it ricochet off the men's room door marked "Cow Pokes."

As you dismount, you get a standing ovation from the patrons. Hopefully, you proved your point: Hitting a golf ball isn't easy!

In their book *The Dynamics of Skill Acquisition: A Constraints-Led Approach* (2008), Keith Davids, Chris Button, and Simon Bennet assert that skill acquisition involves chaos, disorder, and complexity. Contrary to what most golfers think, your brain can't store—then retrieve on demand—*dynamic* swing components such as the pivot, arm movement, and leg drive. However, your brain can store and retrieve on demand *static* swing components such as grip, stance, and posture.

Davids, Button, and Bennet insist that three types of constraints, namely *organismic*, *task*, and *environmental* variables, make every swing slightly different. *Organismic* constraints refer to variables associated with a golfer's physical and mental state, for example arthritic knees or competitive tension. *Task* constraints refer to variables associated with completing a difficult chore such as draining a ten-foot putt or hitting a 250-yard straight drive. *Environmental* constraints refer to variables associated with course conditions like downhill lies, water hazards, and 20-mph winds.

Constraint variables, especially in target-directed sports like golf, tennis, and baseball, affect the skill-acquisition process.

In many respects, variability (i.e., loading your muscles and body parts differently for each shot) helps you avoid injury.

Research findings confirm that expert golfers have the ability to reduce the amount of body movement, clubhead speed, face angle, hand path, and attack angle at the moment of impact. These findings confirm the notions that Bobby Clampett advances in his book *The Impact Zone: Mastering the Moment of Truth.*

Having studied the precepts and swings of David Duvall, Mike Austin, and Mike Dunaway, I changed my thinking. I adopted a so-called "casting" motion in my downswing to release lag from the top.

To minimize the variables in your downswing, use an impact bag to practice keeping the clubhead slightly behind the ball and square to the target. Consistency matters most at impact. Therefore, keep rehearsing your impact position.

Spraying and Praying

Jack Lewis, a decorated USMC veteran of three wars and editor of *Gun World*, maintained that the M1 rifle has significantly degraded combat operations. "The United States used to be known as a Nation of Riflemen," Lewis said, "Now we've become a Nation of Sprayers."

Spraying and praying, a derisive military term that originated during the Rhodesian Bush War (1964–1967), denotes the practice of untrained troops—bereft of proper training and without making any effort to line up their shots—firing scattered and unfocused bursts at the enemy. Golfers, does this sound familiar?

Spraying and praying—the act of untrained troops firing scattered and unfocused shots—characterizes the erratic play of today's poorly trained golfer whose average score is 95 for 18 holes. The game's inherent complexity invites spraying and praying. Golfers swing a 4-inch metal clubhead—attached to a 4-foot steel rod—to hit a ball 1.68 inches in diameter into a 4.25-inch-diameter hole that's often 500 yards away and separated by woods, heavy rough, water hazards, and sand traps.

A swing lasting approximately 1.4 seconds involves most of your body's joints, muscles and bones. To orchestrate the nuanced and precise movement of interrelated body parts, you

19

need world-class timing and coordination. To hit seven successful shots for every ten, you need endless hours of practice. It's perfectly understandable, therefore, that most golfers spray and pray.

Furthermore, golf requires a variety of techniques using fourteen different clubs and under variable conditions in which no two shots are ever the same. Golf movements, unlike those of running, are more complex. Even the best golfers can't perform on autopilot. Golf demands a high level of expert planning, decision making and problem solving. Under constant pressure, you must maintain your composure for an 18-hole, four-hour round or sometimes for a 72-hole, four-day tournament involving hundreds of shots.

During the swing, different parts of your body move in different *directions*, at different *times*, and at different *speeds*. These variables complicate learning. Here's a perfect illustration.

Researchers analyzing the swings of Tour pros recently discovered that their toes rotate as much as 30 mph faster than their heels through the impact zone. This 30-mph differential increases their driving distance by over 30 yards. In other words, learning to rotate your toes and heels into impact at the *same* speed is relatively easy. However, learning to rotate your toes 30-mph *faster* than your heels into impact is extremely difficult.

Spraying denotes sending out bullets, golf balls, emails, or marketing brochures with little forethought and minimal effort. *Praying* means hoping to achieve your desired result. Spray-and-pray golfers are wasting their time.

The Three Stages

Charles Barkley, the former NBA star, has perhaps the world's worst golf swing. When people view Barkley's swing, they avert their eyes. Noted PGA instructor Hank Haney spent a full season trying to remediate Barkley's frightening swing. Haney—who later confessed that he needed a lifetime to fix Barkley's swing—finally gave up. If Barkley's golf swing were a patient, it would be in hospice care.

A superior, conditioned, and agile athlete who lacks specific performance skills is like a Maserati with flat tires. Athletic or motor skills designed to achieve complex tasks are taught and learned in progressive stages.

Skills and abilities are slightly different. A skill—like using watercolors to paint a landscape—denotes employing knowledge, experience, and training to perform a difficult task. An ability—like seeing the beauty in a stunning landscape—denotes using your innate and genetic capacities as the foundation for your skills.

In their book *Human Performance*, Paul Fitts and Michael Posner introduced a learning model consisting of three stages: the *cognitive*, *associative*, and *autonomous*. There is no definitive point when you transition from one stage to the next.

In the *cognitive or verbal* stage, you focus on exactly what you need to do. This stage involves overt self-talk. During this stage, you process information and experiment freely with different approaches using instruction, guidance, slow-motion drills, video analysis, augmented feedback, and other coaching techniques. During the cognitive stage, you ingest and organize information into a meaningful program.

During this stage, you employ consciously controlled, step-by-step movements that induce slow, abrupt, awkward, and inefficient movement patterns. In the cognitive stage, you can hit two or three good shots for every ten.

In the *associative* or *practice* stage, you've already made subtle adjustments to your movement patterns that allow you to perform more consistently, economically, and reliably. Based on kinesthetic feedback and intensive practice, your movement patterns have become more automatic and subconscious.

During the associative phase, sports psychologist Jeffrey Huber writes, "Highly successful athletes and highly successful coaches are always looking for ways to get better. Consequently, they frequently revisit the cognitive stage and the associative phase. Revisiting these stages is the relearning process." At this stage, you can hit five or six good shots for every ten.

In the *autonomous* or *motor* stage, your movements after years of practice are stored in your long-term memory. Your movements have finally become more consistent. Huber writes, ". . . motor movement performance becomes largely automatic, where cognitive processing demands are minimal and athletes are capable of attending to and processing other information, such as the position of other players, game strategy, or the form or style of movement." At this stage, you can hit seven to nine good shots for every 10.

Unfortunately, few golfers manage to advance beyond the associative stage. In golf instruction, there are no absolutes.

Every static and dynamic aspect of swing is fraught with contradictions and controversy.

Your job is to solve golf's underlying problem—synchronizing the turning of your body *and* the swinging of your arms—in whatever way you can. When you solve that problem, you're home free.

Without accurate, verifiable, and scientific information, you can't successfully complete the cognitive stage of your three-part learning process. You must decide which methodology to adopt given the wide range of models, approaches, theories, and practices contained in books, manuals, articles, and videos advanced by noted Tour pros, coaches, instructors, and mentors.

Golf instruction, unlike the martial arts, is not "codified." In the martial arts, pupils learn universally accepted methods of kicking, punching, and blocking. Admittedly, there are different forms of martial arts. But each martial art form is codified.

Similarly, American law school students learn federal laws codified to ensure clarity, standardization, and uniformity among all fifty states. For example, the federal statutes on kidnapping apply nationwide. The *rules* of golf are codified—but not the *techniques and principles* associated with teaching and learning swing mechanics.

Unlike Charles Barkley, you'll optimize your skills when you push through all three stages and perform autonomously.

Engrams

You're on the patio grilling steaks when your nasty mother-in-law strolls over. She's wearing her goofy Mickey Mouse sun visor. Famous for sticking her nose where it doesn't belong, she admonishes you for screwing up the grill marks.

Grill marks on steaks, according to her, are supposed to crisscross. Yours don't. She learned about grill marks from her Uncle Buddy, who owned a meat market in Hoboken. Unlike her, you've forgotten most of the useless shit you learned as a child.

The less your mother-in-law knows, the more she knows it. She claims that making correct grill marks is permanently etched in her brain. In your mother-in-law's feeble brain, there's a memory trace about grill marks.

When memory takes root, your brain theoretically leaves an *engram* or chemical trace. Your brain—containing over 86 billion interconnected neurons or brain cells—leaves physical and chemical memory traces. Without these memory traces, for example, you wouldn't be able to recite the alphabet, name the state capitals, or recall your last three addresses.

Engrams explain *why* selected memories persist and *how* memories are stored. Scientists, however, do not understand exactly how engrams work and where they're located in the brain.

Researchers Matthew Crossely, George Ashby, and Todd Maddox ("Erasing the Engram") assert that the engrams located in your brain's neural pathways are sustained and protected by a thin myelin coating that helps you process thoughts, behaviors, and images. If you want to change your grip, stance, or tempo, for example, you can't simply replace your old neural pathways for new ones. It's not that easy.

To make a swing change, you must create new neural pathways that overwrite old and unwanted neural pathways. Simply put, you learn and support new skills and habits by merging old and new neural pathways. *Relearning* is analogous to building a new house on a preexisting foundation. When you first learned to play golf, you had little or no foundation. Therefore, you had to build your neural pathways and connections (i.e., your foundation) from scratch.

Neuroscience, the study of neural pathways associated with learning, unlearning, and relearning, is very important to golfers. When you learn swing mechanics, you create and strengthen pathways to create pulses of energy that span tiny gaps called synapses.

To learn a new movement pattern, you must generate electrical signals that jump across synaptic gaps and form connections. Generating new neural pathways requires focus and will-power. The more neural pathways you create, the more familiar your movement patterns become.

Learning to ride a bike was once a daunting task. Before you could ride, you needed training wheels and someone to assist you. After a few days of practice, you could ride without consciously thinking about steering and pedaling. When you learned to ride a bike, you developed a lasting mental blueprint or engram. Because engrams take root over time, learning new skills is always easier when you're young.

To swing a club effectively and consistently, you need an engram. However, building the right engram by triggering the correct neural pathways and making the right synaptic connections is extremely difficult, especially later in life. If you've been swinging incorrectly for many years, for example, by using familiar and instinctive muscle movements borrowed from baseball, then you've developed an engram that may be sabotaging your growth. The ability to recognize and replace self-destructive habits is a precious skill.

To improve your game, you must replace your old and useless engrams. To replace your existing engrams, be prepared to expend considerable effort. In *Your Brain at Work*, Dr. David Rock discusses the biological limits and strains associated with changing the structure and function of your brain to enhance your performance. Be advised that consciously holding a new swing thought in your brain requires tremendous energy. Your brain requires an abundant supply of oxygenated blood to make swing changes.

Educated Hands

Ernest Jones, a pioneering golf instructor, lost his right leg below the knee from a grenade burst during WWI. Sent back to recuperate in England, Jones worried his professional golf career was over. Walking on crutches, he shot an 83 during his initial round as an amputee at Royal Norwich in 1916. Several weeks later, he shot a 72 on a longer and more challenging course. His injury forced him to revolutionize his thinking about the golf swing.

Jones developed and taught a simple and effective methodology. After Jones was fitted for a prosthetic in 1923, he became the Head Golf Professional at The Women's National Golf and Tennis Club on Long Island, New York.

During his teaching career, he mentored many world-class golfers, including Virginia Van Wie (winner of 3 consecutive Women's Amateur Championships); Glenna Collette Vare (winner of 49 professional tournaments, including 16 in a row); Lawson Little (winner of 8 PGA tournaments, including the 1940 U.S. Open); Betty Hicks (winner of U.S Women's Open); and Horton Smith (winner of 32 PGA tournaments, including the 1940 and 1942 Masters).

In recognition of Jones's teaching success, PGA officials invited him to deliver the keynote address at their annual convention in 1950. At that time, most PGA instructors gave approximately 600 lessons per year compared to Jones's 3000.

Following his speech, his host contritely informed Jones that the PGA could not possibly endorse his teachings. If the PGA adopted his simple and effective methodology, teaching pros would starve to death. Today, PGA instructors rarely mention Ernest Jones.

Ernest Jones rejected today's *analytical* method of golf instruction. Breaking down the swing part by part, according to Ernest Jones, destroys its rhythmic and holistic nature.

Bobby Jones, perhaps America's greatest golfer, also criticized the PGA's analytical teaching and learning protocols. Bobby Jones viewed the swing as a holistic, unified, dynamic, and continuous back-and-forth motion akin to a pendulum on a grandfather clock. Jones said, "The hands form the connecting link by which the forces brought to life in the player's body are transmitted to the clubhead." Although Jones swung the club with both hands, his left hand played the leading role.

Ron Frankel—an Ernest Jones disciple who operates the Frankel Golf Academy in Palm City, Florida—still teaches the methodology Ernest Jones outlined in his book *Swing the Clubhead* (1937).

On his website, Ron Frankel states, "A golfer must be given the correct key to unlock golf's great mystery. *Golf's One Motion* gives you that key and stops the insanity of constant contradiction, positions, and mechanical quick fixes that are here today and gone tomorrow." A unified pendulum motion, according to Frankel, promotes rhythm, timing, acceleration, balance, centrifugal force, and a repeatable arc.

Ernest Jones urged golfers to "educate" their hands. Jones wrote, ". . . the hands are the medium which controls the swing, with body parts—arms, legs, shoulders and such— performing as admirable followers. Let your body align and support your hands to swing the clubhead at the ball."

Nerve fibers—your body's information messengers—transmit sensory data from your arms to your fingertips. In a *PubMed* article, "How Does the Hand Work?" the author states, "The movements of the arms must be fast, precise, and strong to complete the diverse activities the body engages in throughout the day. Even the tiny hand muscles, which perform very delicate and precise movements, are driven by about 200,000 neurons."

According to Dr. Wilder Penfield (in "The Cerebral Cortex of Man"), one quarter of your brain's motor cortex controls the muscles in your hands. Rapid nerve signals between your brain and hands facilitate precise and intricate movements.

Literally and figuratively, grasping is synonymous with understanding. The words "concept" and "precept" are derived from the Latin root *capere*, meaning to grasp, seize, or hold.

Observe what happens when you place a rattle in a baby's crib. The baby, equipped with billions of active neurons, will immediately grasp the rattle. Babies use their hands to construct their world.

Infants employ their mirror neurons for imitative learning. Before infants learn to smile, according to researchers, they learn to stretch out their hands to grasp things. After two weeks, babies start grasping for toy rattles and their mother's finger.

Cognitive scientists refer to the mental process of using your hands for learning as "neurophysiological weaving." The secret to mastering complex swing mechanics resides in the untapped domain of neurophysiology.

When your hands contact your physical reality, you fabricate a personal and internal tapestry on the multidimensional loom of your mind. In sum, your hands weave a subtle reality inside your brain.

In *The Brain That Changes Itself*, Dr. Norman Doidge—a Canadian psychiatrist—offers a fascinating glimpse of the current revolution in neuroscience. Dr. Doidge relates a study in which students learning to play a series of notes on a piano experience changes in their brain's electrical activity. Furthermore, students who sit in front of a piano and contemplate playing a series of notes—compared to those who actually play the piano—experience the same changes in their brain's electrical activity. In other words, your brain can make the virtual—real.

Neurobiologist Dr. Peter Strick claims that the area of the brain responsible for hand movements, namely, the primary motor cortex, is larger among professional pianists than amateur pianists. His observation suggests that extensive practice induces dramatic changes in one's primary motor cortex. MRI studies demonstrate that "educating" your hands makes awkward and forced movements—smooth and natural.

Neurologist Matti Bergström, who refers to the hands as "the eyes of the brain," asserts that millions of nerve endings in the finger tips provide the hands with unique learning skills.

On his website, neurophysiologist Professor Bergström states: "The brain discovers what the fingers explore . . . If we don't use our fingers, if in childhood we become *finger blind,* the rich network of nerves is impoverished, which represents a huge loss to the brain and thwarts the individual's all round development."

Arthur and Elizabeth Auer, in *Learning About the World Through Modeling* (2013), provide an historical context for hands-on learning: "Through the fact that man is an upright being and his hands are thus freed from resting on the earth, they have become, down through the ages, the most marvelous instruments. . . . Through infinite variations of all these, it has become one of man's most creative and, at the same time, selfless organs."

Rudolf Steiner, in *Rhythms of Learning* (1998), maintained that the hands are "the eyes of the rhythmic system."

Steiner asserted that the rhythmic use of your hands, starting from childhood, makes brain cells highly receptive to "living thoughts." Your hands as rhythmic sensors allow ideas to come alive. The receptors in your hands can apprehend the swing's exquisite rhythm and tempo.

Dr. Frank Wilson, a prominent neurologist, claims the human hand is a miracle of biomechanics. Wilson offers some startling and relevant insights in his book *The Hand: How It Shapes the Brain, Language and Culture* (1998). Wilson refers to his book as "a meditation on the human hand, born of nearly two decades of personal and professional experiences." Wilson, whose observations are directly applicable to learning the golf swing, criticizes the traditional and narrow brain-centered view of intelligence.

According to Wilson, humans must *merge hand and brain* to attain knowledge and understanding. Dr. Wilson writes, "The brain does not live inside the head, even though that is its formal habitat. It reaches out to the body, and with the body it reaches out to the world. The brain is the hand, and the hand is the brain." The ongoing interaction between head and hands, according to Wilson, reshapes the brain and vitalizes learning. Your hands are your "outer brain."

The hands are vital components in the swing's complex system. What matters most in a system are the connections and interactions among its components—not the components themselves. To educate your hands, you must understand how they function systemically. In other words, examine how your hands act separately AND interact holistically. Your hands—your only contact with the club—are directly and indirectly related to everything else in your swing.

To educate your hands, use a ruler to represent a golf club. Grip the ruler in your trailing hand. Assume your address position and point the ruler downward. Applying a downward force on the butt end with the heel pad of your palm, vertically invert the ruler so it stands up and down. With the end of the ruler pointing upward, swing the butt end in a tilted circle.

In sum, educate your hands to *swing the entire club . . . at the same time . . . in the same direction . . .* and *at the same speed* in a pendular motion, as Manuel de la Torre famously advised. Golfers who mistakenly bring back the clubhead in a wide, flat arc—whereby the butt end and clubhead move in opposite directions—destroy the swing's pendulum-like movement.

Homer Kelley maintained that the hands in the golf swing function simply as "clamps." This notion, however, is not entirely true. In the backswing, the throwing hand actively counterrotates 90 degrees at the wrist axle and bends back toward your forearm. In the downswing, the hands actively throw the clubhead.

Since all expert swings contain an elusive *active-passive-active* rhythmic sequence, you must educate your hands as if you were a violinist playing a sonata or musical composition performed in three distinct movements.

Educated hands begin at address. Consider setting your hands relatively close to your thighs, then lowering them. Position the butt end of each club below your trouser zipper.

At address, educate your hands to establish the correct lie angle—the orientation of the sole relative to the ground—for each club. For both address and impact, your irons and woods should be slightly "toe up"—not flush with the ground. At address, if you can insert a credit card under the toe and slide it halfway down the sole, you're fine. Don't excessively heel or toe your irons and woods.

For every degree your lie angle at impact is amiss, your ball will stray four yards off-line. For example, if the lie angle of your pitching wedge is four degrees off-center at impact, you'll miss the green by sixteen yards.

Positioning the club slightly "toe up" at address compensates for predictable downswing changes in your hand path and shaft bend (i.e., "droop"). As the clubhead moves *down* and *forward* in your downswing, centrifugal force will pull your hands *inward* and *upward* and bend the shaft three to five degrees. Pulling your hands and club upward at impact—a desirable effect called "parametric acceleration"—speeds up the clubhead.

To achieve machine-like consistency, Hogan maintained the same swing width. Simply put, he set his hands at the top the same distance from his trailing shoulder for every swing. He also kept his lead thumb under his trailing thumb for every shot. Depending on your flexibility, physique, and arm length, try positioning your hands at shoulder height or slightly above and maintaining the same width for every full shot.

In the downswing, educate your hands to set and reset your *lag angle* (i.e., the angle formed between your shaft and lead forearm). When your lead arm is parallel to the ground halfway into your backswing, create a 90-degree lag angle. In transition, however, radially flex your lead wrist (i.e., bend it back toward your lead thumb) to reset your lag angle to 45 degrees. In sum, don't retain a 90-degree lag angle from address to the delivery position. Don't hold lag.

When you reduce your lag angle to 45 degrees in transition by radially flexing your lead wrist, the shaft will move to within four or five inches of your rear shoulder. Performing "The Pump Drill" trains your hands to reduce your lag angle (i.e., from 90 degrees to 45 degrees) and spring-load the shaft in your transition.

Resetting your lag angle in transition enables the club to change directions. During the transition, expert golfers actually move in two directions at once. As their hands and club continue to move *back*, their lower body starts moving *forward*. Hogan protégés, who employ a conventional pivot and move in opposite directions during their transition, squat or "sit down" to lower their center of gravity. Conversely, Mike Austin protégés, who employ a compound pivot, rock their spines during their transition to remain relatively upright. Take your choice.

Educate your hands to maintain a constant swing *radius*. The fixed distance established at address between your sternum slot and hands constitutes your swing radius. Overswinging, which collapses your arms and hands in the backswing, alters your swing radius, reduces clubhead speed, and compromises distance.

Ponder this. To inscribe a circle on paper with a geometric compass, you need a fixed distance or radius between the needle arm and the pencil. Similarly, to create a "circular" swing, you need a fixed distance or radius between your sternum slot and hands. However, unlike a geometry compass with one fixed leg, you swing on two legs. Thus, your backswing and downswing paths are elliptical—not circular. Regardless, envision your swing as a circle.

To establish a proper swing radius, measure the distance between your sternum slot and hands at address. To conceptualize this distance, cut a wooden dowel of similar length. Imagine this dowel—your virtual radius—affixed between your sternum slot and hands throughout your swing.

Mike Austin invented and marketed a training device called "The Flammer." Designed to help golfers maintain a fixed radius, his device consisted of a shoulder harness and a breastplate equipped with an adjustable connecting rod between the sternum slot and hands. To maintain a fixed radius, imagine that you're wearing a "Flammer."

Educate your hands to apply *torque*. Torque denotes a *turning force* directed at the ball—not a *twisting force* directed around the axis of the shaft. Expert golfers use a turning force to direct the entire *club* into the ball. Inept golfers use a twisting force along the axis of the shaft to direct the *clubface* into the ball. Torque the entire club to turn it "around the corner." Don't twist the shaft around its axis to turn just the clubhead.

Swing the club back and forth like a pendulum in a grandfather clock. The mechanism in a grandfather clock that locks and unlocks the pendulum to move back and forth is called the *escapement*. It releases—or lets the pendulum "escape"— by giving it a slight burst of energy to counteract friction and drag. Ideally, club pendulums and clock pendulums should swing back and forth in perfect resonance.

Think of your club as a pendulum. Think of your hands as an escapement mechanism attached to the butt end of your club. Think of moving the butt end first and standing up the club as if it were a buggy whip. Think of moving the butt end in a tilted circle that passes under your Adam's apple and over the base of your neck.

Think of using the bottom bone in your lead wrist as a stable fulcrum to leverage the butt end and swing the pendulum. Think of tracing the butt end—not the clubhead—along two circular paths.

Then hit balls one-handed. Use your lead hand as a stable fulcrum to leverage the butt end. Send the entire club "around the corner" into impact. Point the butt end downward into impact.

Swing the butt end of a rope draped over your trailing shoulder. Use a ½- or ¾-inch nylon rope approximately 50 inches long. Drape it over your trailing shoulder and position your hands at the top. Pin your leading upper arm to your chest wall. Then activate your lower body to rotate your torso, thereby whipping the rope down and through. When you *swing* a rope from the butt end, your hands will swing the entire rope, in the same direction, at the same time and at the same speed. Swing your arms and turn your body in unison.

Swing a hammer from the butt end. Imagine that you're standing upright and pounding a three-foot wooden stake into the ground with a croquet mallet. Keep your hands passive, lift up your arms, and drive the stake into the ground. Don't rotate the shaft of the mallet. Swing the hammer from the butt end.

Activate your hands in the takeaway. Quiet them in the backswing. Activate them again at impact. Retain the angle formed at the base of your thumbs and turn your body without rotating the clubhead or shaft. Use your rear elbow and rear palm to slam down the hammer. Move the butt end of the hammer along a circular path.

Swing an alignment rod or graphite shaft at the butt end to generate clubhead speed. Swing faster and faster to produce loud swishing sounds. Coordinate your hands, arms, and torso.

Ernest Jones wrote, "The body and all its parts should be treated as wholly admirable followers of the action of the hands and fingers. Forget about everything else. You cannot do more than one thing at a time. Don't let your mind and actions flitter. The sooner you understand that you swing the clubhead with your hands . . . the nearer you will be to the perfect swing."

As your hands and arms move the butt end of the pendulum in a tilted circle, swivel your ankles, lift and lower your heels, and pivot on your toes. Educated hands produce educated swings.

Focus

You're physically and mentally drained after your golf lesson at Cheswick's Golf Learning Center, a driving range and soft-serve facility on Route 19. Your instructor, Buddy Cheswick, holds a B.S. (with honors) in biomechanics from Lumpkin State University. After your lesson, your brain, like a Polish sausage, is stuffed with technical swing thoughts.

On the way home you make a pit stop at The Tipsy Moose, where Carmine buys you a beer. When your frosted mug of lager arrives, you pause momentarily to consider your thumb position, wrist cock, elbow bend, arm extension, and spine angle. After your golf lesson, you're biomechanically constipated.

To learn swing mechanics, distinguish between *internal* and *external* focus. *Internal* focus during your swing places your attention on body positions. *External* focus during your swing places your attention on club positions.

Since the advent of TrackMan in 2003, many golfers have adopted *internal focus* as their primary attention mode. TrackMan, developed by an electrical engineer, is a dual-radar device that generates 27 data points associated with the club and ball. Over 150 Tour pros and their coaches employ TrackMan. In fact, a dozen PGA pros employ swing coaches with doctorates in biomechanics and kinesiology. TrackMan is The Holy Grail for instructors whose focus is primarily internal.

Do you recall when you learned to ride a bike? When you shifted your primary focus from operating your *body* to operating your *bike*, you achieved an immediate breakthrough. To improve your swing—a complex and tightly coupled system—consider shifting your focus.

Focusing externally on swinging the club stresses outcomes, automatic movements, and subconscious controls. In an article published in *International Review of Sport and Exercise Physiology*, Dr. Gabriele Wulf, a UNLV research kinesiologist, endorses external focus for athletes engaged in golf, tennis, throwing, ball kicking, rowing, juggling, gymnastics, weightlifting, track and field, swimming, and kayaking.

She writes, "The more complex or challenging the task, the greater the advantages of adopting an external focus. . . . It's been shown to promote automatic movement control and enhancements in all aspects of performance, including movement effectiveness and efficiency."

Decide for yourself which attention mode is more effective. Don't blindly accept the attention mode of others. Dr. Wulf writes, "In decades of research, I've never seen anyone improve by using internal swing thoughts."

If you wrongly focus on swinging the *clubhead*, consider the adverse systemic effects. Your forearms will overrotate and separate, your lead shoulder will elevate in the takeaway, your trailing elbow will move away from your rib cage, your hands will flip at impact, your club will ascribe an out-to-in path, your arms will swing around and across your body, and your head and body will move laterally.

If you properly focus on swinging the *butt end*, consider its beneficial systemic effects. Your hands will move back, up, and in; your lead forearm will be above your trailing forearm in the downswing; your forearms will rotate the correct amount;

your swing plane will become slightly more vertical; and the weight of your clubhead will promote a natural hand action and wrist hinge—not vice versa. Swinging the butt end is a systemic remedy.

Manuel del a Torre, author of *Understanding the Golf Swing* (2001), was an outspoken exponent of external focus. He advised golfers *to swing the entire club in the same direction, at the same time, and at the same rate of speed.*

However, choosing exclusively between internal and external focus is an example of simplistic "dualistic" (i.e., either-or) thinking. Dualistic thinking, the lowest form of cognition, leads to moronic, errant, and impulsive decisions. Don't choose between internal and external. Merge internal and external.

Try initiating your swing by focusing internally on your lead shoulder and externally on the butt end. Turn your lead shoulder—a key source of stability—down, under, and slightly across your body toward your sternum slot *and* point the butt end toward the ball. Starting your swing with your hands and wrists—rather than your lead shoulder—creates serious problems. For example, your shoulders won't turn properly; your hands will take over the action; your club will move inside the target-line; and your tempo will vanish. Concentrating on turning your lead shoulder and pointing the butt end at the ball—two simple focal points—will start your swing correctly, simplify everything, and unclutter your mind.

Merging internal and external focus is also important during your transition. Start your downswing with your upper lead arm pinned to your chest wall. To master the transition—which simultaneously blends internal and external focus—practice repeatedly in slow motion. After hundreds of repetitions, you'll recruit the requisite neural pathways to execute a solid transition.

Choosing between internal and external performance cues is like choosing ice cream or pie for dessert. Exercise integrative or combinational thinking by merging both. Shift between internal focus (e.g., moving your hands, elbows, wrists, pelvis, etc.) *and* external focus (e.g., moving the butt end, shaft, and clubhead).

Performance cues are situational. Rely on internal—or body-focused—performance cues to derive sensory feedback, for example, when you're doing slow-motion drills in a mirror. However, rely on external—or club-focused—performance cues when you're playing and competing. Excessive internal focus during play invites "paralysis by analysis."

Golf and ballet movements involve flowing paths of energy. Ballet dancers and golfers use external focus to create visualizations to trigger subconscious and kinesthetic sensations. Ballet dancers, for example, might visualize themselves trying to catch a wind-blown leaf to achieve flowing hand and arm movements. Or they may visualize lightning bolts emanating from their feet and legs to induce leaping movements. External performance cues, consonant with creative visualizations and kinesthetic sensations, greatly enhance learning.

In *Dance Psychology for Artistic and Performance Excellence* (2015), Jim Taylor and Elena Estanol advise dancers to adopt their own dominant "focus-style" when learning, rehearsing, and performing. A *broad* external focus helps to enhance choreography. Conversely, a *narrow* internal focus helps to refine nuanced individual movements. However, all expert dancers exhibit focus-flexibility.

Use external focus, augmented by creative visualizations and kinesthetic sensations, to develop a spontaneous and rhythmic swing. Nick Bradley's bestselling book, *Kinetic Golf: Picture the Game Like Never Before* (2013), features over one hundred dramatic visualizations that simplify complex anatomical movements, actualize kinesthetic learning, and promote breakthroughs.

When you have a beer at The Tipsy Moose, use external focus. See the mug . . . grab the mug . . . lift the mug . . . drink the beer.

Structure

Mario totally stressed out when his mother-in-law moved into his basement apartment. Yesterday, he woke up screaming before he realized he wasn't even asleep. Undue stress has prompted Mario to tighten his grip and quicken his tempo.

Vinnie, who can't leave sick enough alone, advised Mario to grip the club as if he were holding a canary. Now Mario's loosey-goosey swing lacks structure.

Infusing selected pressures and forces into key muscles and joints during setup is the best and quickest way to achieve a balanced, structured, consistent, and powerful swing.

There is considerable variability in the movements of expert golfers. However, there is little variability in their structure and balance of their movements. The *dynamic* components of the swing are difficult to master. However, the *static* components of the setup—once properly understood—are easy to master. Focus first on the static elements.

Structure denotes the connection and arrangement of components in a complex system. In complex systems the *connections* between components—not the components themselves—are most important.

Breakdowns occur in complex systems when connections are either too tight or too loose. *Interference* and *clearance* are engineering terms that denote degrees of tightness or loose-ness among the couplings or connections in a complex sys-tems. For example, the couplings that transfer torque between a turbine's shaft and a turbine must be flexible—neither too tight nor too loose.

It's the same thing with your swing. Your body's 360 joints connect and allow individual bones to move. Your swing will break down if your joints are too tight or too loose. Generally speaking, loose swing couplings are better than tight swing couplings. To generate the requisite amount of torque and power, your swing couplings or joints require different degrees of looseness and tightness.

Percy Boomer, who won the Swiss, Dutch, and Belgian Opens during the 1920s, took a *systems approach* to learning and mastering the golf swing. In his seminal book *On Learning Golf* (1946), Boomer used the term "muscle memory" to con-vey the idea that golfers must repeat the same intrinsic sensa-tion for every shot based on a uniformly structured swing.

Accordingly, Boomer advised golfers to structure their swing during the setup by *bracing*—or applying pressure and directional forces—to three key areas. Boomer writes, "The first is the *inwards* brace, applying to the hips, elbows, shoul-ders, and stomach. The second is the *upwards* brace of our bod-ies, which makes us feel down and firm on our feet. The third direction of brace [i.e., *sideways*] is a twist around of our hips to the left. The right knee does not resist, so we find our left side straight and right side bowed inwards. To complete the set, the head and chin should be turned slightly to the right." Boomer urged his pupils to "swing in a barrel" to prevent their hips from sliding laterally. Many experts disagree with Boomer on this point.

PGA instructor Jimmy Ballard, golf's "Pioneer of Connection," has urged golfers to tighten the couplings in their swings. In *How to Perfect Your Golf Swing: Using Connection and the Seven Common Denominators* (1981), Ballard asserts that great ball-strikers regardless of sport—including Arthur Ashe in tennis, Joe DiMaggio in baseball, and Ben Hogan in golf—share one essential quality: connection.

Ballard maintains that *connection*—linking the small muscles of the arms and the larger muscles of the shoulders, torso, and legs—governs the golf swing. Ballard's precepts are based on systems theory.

Ballard advises golfers at setup to *connect* their arms and body by squeezing their elbows together, positioning their elbow pockets skyward, pinching in their shoulder blades, and "plugging in" their upper arms below the shoulder sockets or armpits from address to impact.

Sam Byrd—a former Yankee slugger and successful PGA professional—learned the "secret of connection" from Babe Ruth, who advised him to swing a bat as if he had a towel tucked under his left or lead armpit. Sam Byrd later shared this secret with both Ben Hogan and Jimmy Ballard. Staying connected—using a so-called "shoulder-pinch" or "pec-grab"—applies whether you're swinging a baseball bat, tennis racket, or golf club. *Pinning your upper lead arm to your chest wall—thereby connecting your arms and torso—is perhaps golf's biggest secret.*

Ben Hogan in *The Five Lessons: The Modern Fundamentals of Golf* (1957) instructs golfers to structure their swings by resting their upper arms lightly against their chest wall throughout the swing. Hogan's right arm moved slightly away at the top of his backswing; however, it fell nicely back into place as he started his forward swing. By keeping his upper lead arm close to his body and bending his elbows—using "half-arms"—Hogan maintained a fixed radius and a consistent swing plane.

Forming a *power triangle* with his arms, shoulder girdle, and hands, Hogan kept his elbows together as he turned his shoulders and rotated his torso. Hogan used a structured triangle and connected components to generate power and consistency.

Percy Boomer, Jimmy Ballard, and Ben Hogan advised golfers to position their lead elbow downward during the swing. Simply stated, they emphasized the "downness" of the lead elbow. Hogan likened the motion of keeping his left elbow down and lead thumb up during the swing to that of "hitching a ride."

To structure your setup, apply three specific pressures. Employ *elbow pressure* to connects the arms, shoulders, and torso to the two upper points of the triangle. Employ *grip pressure* to connect the hands and club to the lower point of the triangle. Employ *pivot pressure* to connect the feet, legs, and hips to balance and stabilize the power triangle.

Elbow pressure connects your arms, shoulders, and torso to two, fixed, upper points of your power triangle. Train your trailing elbow to point downward. Elbow structure induces shoulder structure. Often instructors advise their pupils to swing with a soccer ball placed between their elbows. Ensure that the ball's diameter matches the distance between your connected elbows. As you swing, hold the ball in place with your elbows. If the ball drops, your elbows have separated, couplings have loosened, and the power triangle has collapsed. You can hit long and powerful shots without connecting your elbows. However, you can't do it consistently.

Grip pressure connects your hands and club to the bottom point of your power triangle. Maintaining constant grip pressure is a daunting task. Sam Snead used the phrase "playing the flute" to describe how most golfers' fingers separate from the club and alter their grip during the swing. Hogan advised golfers to grip the club firmly using the bottom three fingers of the lead hand, thereby allowing them to "scroll" the handle.

Hogan learned to maintain steady grip pressure by hitting multiple practice balls without removing his hands from the club between shots. Try this. Or try swinging by maintaining fixed contact with a shoelace interwoven among the handle, fingers, thumbs, and palms. Bottom line: maintain constant grip pressure.

Pivot pressure provides your power triangle with a stable base. Many golfers mistakenly believe they need lots of leg and hip movement to shift their weight. Actually, undue hip and leg movement promotes excessive hip sliding and shoulder tilting. To structure your lower body at setup, create an *A-shape* or lower triangle formed by your feet, legs, and hips. Gently press your thighs together and bow out your knees a fraction of an inch. Standing slightly bowlegged—compared to standing slightly knock-kneed—affords you greater stability and balance.

Bowlegged cowboys have greater stability in their knees. Your car will wobble when the lug nuts are loose. Your swing will wobble if your knees are loose.

Maintaining the flex in your trailing knee throughout your swing—one of golf's well-kept secrets—gives you stability, resistance, and power. With a structured trailing knee, you can't pivot and shift your weight.

Maintain the A-shape until impact by ensuring (1) that neither leg moves perpendicular to the ground and (2) that neither shoulder moves outside its respective hip. Sustaining your A-shape will keep your upper body between your feet, tighten your pivot, compact your swing, prevent leaning, and enhance your balance.

Ball Flight Laws

Knowledge keeps changing. Aristotle, having realized that ships disappear over the horizon, proposed that the world was *round*. Isaac Newton, having realized that ocean levels are deeper at the equator, proposed that the Earth was a *squashed* sphere. Vic Baker, a University of Arizona geologist, having realized that the planet's surface is mountainous and its core unevenly distributed, proposed that the Earth resembles a *bumpy, spinning, slightly deformed sphere of Silly Putty*. Contrary to what astronauts famously claimed, the Earth is not a "blue marble."

Generations of golf professionals have long assumed that *club path* dictates your shot's initial direction and that the *club-face* dictates your shot's curvature. This underlying assumption—crucial to how golf is taught and learned—is programmed into the software of golf simulators and minds of instructors. Based on recent scientific tests, this assumption is dead wrong.

Large ideas change slowly. Small ideas change rapidly. All information—like dairy products—has an expiration date.

In his book *The Half-Life of Facts: Why Everything We Know Has an Expiration Date* (2011), Samuel Abresman uses the term *the churning of knowledge* to characterize our changing information-landscape. To cope with uncertainty, realize that knowledge keeps changing.

Abresman cites a study conducted by a team of physicians at a Paris hospital. Abresman asked a medical team, whose specialty was liver disorders, to do two things: (1) to examine 500 journal articles on cirrhosis and hepatitis published within the last 50 years and (2) to rate each article's findings as *factual*, *out-of-date*, or *disproven*. His study revealed that over 50 percent of the medical articles contained *dated* or *disproven* information.

Abresman claims that approximately 50 percent of the findings in most medical journals have a shelf life of fewer than 45 years. Accordingly, medical school faculty tell students that the information they're learning will be obsolete soon after they graduate.

According to Abresman, physics textbooks become outdated in 13.07 years, math textbooks in 9.17 years, psychology textbooks in 7.15 years, and history textbooks in 7.13 years. Unfortunately, Abresman's study didn't include golf books.

We're constantly being bombarded with new and contradictory information. Keeping abreast of rapidly changing information is impossible. When overwhelming evidence supports a new and radical theory, cognitive shifts occur only when the majority of experts finally accept it. Physicist Max Planck wrote, "A new scientific truth does not triumph by convincing its opponents and making them see the light, but rather because its opponents eventually die and a new generation grows up that is familiar with it."

Golfers often ignore and reject new and contradictory information. To improve your swing, remain open-minded and stay current.

John Jacobs, a legendary golf instructor, based his teaching philosophy on "The Laws of Ball Flight." In *Practical Golf* (1972), Jacobs claims there are nine possible ball flights congruent with two sets of variables: (1) whether the club path relative to the target line is *in-to-out*, *square-to-square*, or *out-to-in* and (2) whether the clubface at impact is *closed*, *open*, or *square*.

Jacobs asserted (1) that *club path* dictates whether your shot will hook, slice, pull, push, push-slice, push-hook, pull-hook, pull-slice, or fly straight and (2) that *clubface angle* at impact dictates how much your shot will curve left or right. Today, The US Golf School Organization and many top instructors teach these ball flight laws. However, these laws no longer stand up.

In January 2009, TrackMan's Newsletter published an article titled "The Secret of the Straight Shot." Researchers—using Doppler Radar launch monitors and high-speed cameras—established that the *clubface*—not the *club path*—is the main determinant of ball flight.

According to the *old* ball flight laws, club path and clubface contribute equally in determining ball flight. *The PGA Teaching Manual* (2002)—currently used by 27,000 PGA professionals to foster effective teaching and learning at all levels—promulgates these incorrect laws.

According to the *new* ball flight laws, the clubface contributes approximately 85 percent to ball flight. Club path contributes only 15 percent to ball flight. The slower the clubhead moves through the impact area, the more it affects the ball's launch and spin.

Ball flight laws are crucial in understanding why you're pulling, slicing, or fading. Equipped with inaccurate information, instructors will mistakenly conclude that your pull slices (i.e., shots that start left and curve back to the right) are caused not only by your out-to-in club path, but also by your open club face at impact. Consequently, you'll obediently alter your club path and square up your clubface. Wrong!

To improve my ball-striking, I struggled to find the right combination of club path and clubface. When I accessed current information, I realized my mistake. My club path was perfectly correct. What was incorrect was my clubface at impact. I needed to fix only one component in my tightly coupled complex system: my clubface at impact. To fix your swing, you need factual information.

The swing's complex system is baffling enough without experts promulgating false, subjective, and unscientific information. Recent technological advances prove that the *old* ball flight laws are incorrect.

Most golfers are not in an *information vacuum—but* in a *truth vacuum.* It's not that golfers know too little. It's that they know too much that isn't true.

You don't need a TrackMan Monitor to hit straight shots. Rather, make your own device to monitor your clubface at impact. First, order online a package of nickel-size magnets. Second, glue three magnets together in a stack. Third, glue the end of an 8-inch wooden dowel atop the stack. Fourth, attach your device to the sweet spot located 3 to 5 grooves from the bottom of the clubface. Fifth, perform slow-motion drills to *eye-track* the dowel to attain the optimum impact position of clubface and ball. To square up your clubface at impact, most importantly, aim the dowel at the *bottom of your swing arc*—or approximately four inches beyond the ball—not at the *back of the ball.* Got it?

To become your own expert, remain vigilant. The golf information you learned years ago may no longer abide. Knowledge keeps churning. To become your own expert, surf the Internet, refresh your thinking, identify blind spots, and self-correct.

When Mario's son conveyed what Mrs. Globczak mentioned in class that dinosaurs once had feathers and that Twinkies go bad after 45 days, Mario retorted: "Did Mrs. Globczak also tell your class that the Earth is as flat as the back of Uncle Carmine's head?"

Rocking and Throwing

When Rory McIlroy on the par-5 eighth hole of the 2015 World Golf Championship at Trump National Doral hit his second shot into the water, he blew a fuse. He threw his Nike 3-iron so far into the water that his caddie, J.P Fitzgerald, couldn't retrieve it. Rory played the final ten holes with only 13 clubs and finished his round at even par.

When Rory hit his ball into the water, he used a *hitting* motion. When Rory hurled his 3-iron into the water, he used a *throwing* motion. *Hitting* the ball and *throwing* at the target—different motions—produce different effects.

In fact, Fred Shoemaker in *Extraordinary Golf* (1996) recommends club-throwing drills to train students to swing toward the target. When Shoemaker instructs his students to throw their clubs underhand at a target down range, he removes the ball from their consciousness. By simply changing their intent from *hitting* to *throwing*, Shoemaker's students experience dramatic and sudden improvement. Throwing clubs down range underhanded trains you to rotate your wrist axles by using a clockwise motion similar to turning a crank or scooping ice cream.

Harvey Penick in his *Little Red Book* (1992) doesn't mention a throwing motion. However, Penick does advise golfers to "take dead aim," namely, to banish all thoughts except selecting a target and aiming at it. Penick wanted golfers to fixate on the *target*—not the *ball*.

Ben Hogan in *The Five Lessons* (1957) compares swinging a club to throwing a baseball sidearm, skipping a stone across a pond, and tossing a medicine ball with both hands.

Mike Austin—"The Leonardo Da Vinci of Golf"—advised golfers to throw the club at the target by tilting their spine more and rotating their hips less. Many decades later, Mike Bennett and Andy Plummer based their "Stack and Tilt" system (except for the issue of weight distribution during the swing) on Austin's model. Scientists confirm that Austin's swing—considered the longest and straightest—places very little stress on the joints. Mike Austin, who held a doctorate in kinesiology, was well ahead of his time.

Einstein once said that if he had only one hour to solve a problem, he would spend 59 minutes defining it. Most experts define the swing problem as follows: *How to blend seamlessly the swinging motion of the arms and the turning motion of the torso.* To solve this problem, try rocking your spine and throwing the club underhand as if you were a fast-pitch softball hurler.

To execute holistic and dynamic movements, athletes must remain "connected." To remain connected, practice hitting shots with a golf glove tucked under only your lead armpit. Connect your *lead arm*. Pretend that your lead shoulder is in a sling. Then initiate your forward swing with your lower body to engage your shoulder girdle and fling your arms.

Adopting biomechanics associated with hitting a baseball, as many golfers do, won't help your golf swing. Baseball and golf are deceptively different. In golf you *swing a* pendulum. In baseball you *leverage a* bat. In golf you throw the club *underhand*. In baseball you throw the ball *overhand*. In golf your swing path—like a Ferris wheel—is more vertical. In baseball your hitting path—like a carousel—is more horizontal.

To execute your takeaway, pretend you're throwing a football. In the address position, hold the football in your throwing hand and observe what happens: You'll counterrotate your hand 90 degrees and flex your palm (i.e., ball your hand into a fist). Next you'll fold and retract your elbow and lift your arm to shoulder height. That's what your throwing hand does in the takeaway. To complete your backswing, turn your torso to swing your arms, connected under your armpits, to shoulder height.

In golf, you *rock your spine and shoulders*. In baseball, you *swing around your spine with your shoulders*. A golf club has a flat hitting surface with *one tiny sweet spot*. A baseball bat has a cylindrical hitting surface with multiple *sweet spots*. Therefore, swinging a club and swinging a bat—two very different implements—require different biomechanical motions.

How would you hit a baseball if your bat had a pea-sized sweet spot on a flat surface? Would you roll your forearms, loosen your wrists, and flip your hands? Golfers conditioned by baseball must *unlearn* their incorrect movement patterns and *relearn* correct ones.

Employ analogies to *simplify the complex* and *familiarize the strange*. Dudley Malone, an American attorney and politician, wrote, "One good analogy is worth three hours of conversation." Jack Nicklaus made use of vivid mental images—what he called "going to the movies"—to hone his talents.

To throw the club underhand with your trailing arm, visualize how fast-pitch softball hurlers rock their hips, shoulders, and spine. After your forward press, start your backswing by rocking the base of your spine (i.e., coccyx) away from the target and tilting your front shoulder downward.

In your forward swing, rock the base of your spine toward the target as you tilt your front shoulder upward. Don't rotate around your spine. Tilt and rock your body's six pairs of levers in your ankles, knees, hips, elbows, wrists, and shoulders to energize your throwing motion. Mike Austin preached, "*Mobility—not stability.*"

Rocking your spine shifts your weight but keeps your head between your feet. Conversely, rotating around your spine shifts your weight and moves you off the ball. If there's no need to move off the ball, why do it? Suppose you had only 1.4 seconds to aim and fire a rifle at a target. Would you move off the target, resight it, then shoot? Throwing *underhand* steadies your head. Throwing *overhand* moves your head.

Swing your spine as if it were a clapper in a church bell. While the headstock of the bell remains still, the crown or shoulders of the bell tilt, and the clapper (i.e., your arms and club) moves like a pendulum. Now the bottom of the clapper (i.e., your coccyx), moving from side to side, can strike the rim of the bell. The rim of the bell doesn't rotate around the fixed axis of the clapper. Rather, the rim of the bell rocks and tilts to move the pendular clapper from side to side. To ring the bell, rock your hips beneath your head.

Swinging around the axis of your spine and turning your shoulders horizontally—consonant with conventional teaching—induces back injuries and inconsistent ball-striking. From a system's perspective, one wrong piece of advice—like rotating around the axis of your spine—will sabotage your swing.

Since your spine is not your swing axis, rotate your tilted shoulders around an imaginary diagonal axis that runs from your target ear, passes through your sternum, and exits near your upper rear thigh.

A rocking or tilting motion—as Mike Austin advised— harnesses ground forces, promotes proper footwork, enhances your rhythm, creates an energy spiral, connects your arms and torso, keeps the club on plane, and allows you to throw underhand as fast and hard as you want.

Mike Austin compared lifting, retracting, and loading your trailing elbow and arm in the *backswing* to that of a quarterback preparing to throw a pass. Skilled golfers and quarterbacks point their trailing elbow downward. PGA instructor Bobby Lopez compares the weight shift, hip rotation, and arm- flinging movements in your *downswing* to that of an Olympian throwing a discus. *Throw the club by rotating your lower body as if you were flinging a Frisbee with your upper lead arm securely pinned to your chest.*

Throwing activities—such as darts, archery, and horseshoes—are target-based. *Hitting* activities—such as tennis, baseball, and golf—are object-based. Andrew Hilts, a top PGA instructor, states, "It's all about swinging through the ball—not to it." Hilts claims it's easier for golfers to attain the correct impact-fix by focusing on a *motion* rather than on a *position*.

First, an underhand and rocking throwing motion enhances your *balance*. Make balance—the key to consistency, distance, and accuracy—your priority. Staying in balance in the performance of dynamic and complex skills is an art form. You have three sensory systems to enhance your balance: the vestibular system (i.e., inner ear), ocular system (i.e., eyes) and proprioception (i.e., spatial awareness).

These input systems—designed to coordinate and execute complex throwing movements—allowed our primitive ancestors to survive by hurling lethal stones and spears. It's easier to establish a balanced *throwing* position than a balanced *hitting* position. Moving your pelvis from side to side *balances* and *counterbalances* your swing.

Second, an underhand and rocking throwing motion enhances your *release*. A 2017 study titled "Optimum Strategies for Throwing Accuracy" conducted by a team of Yale physicists has relevant implications for golfers. Examining why certain throwing motions work better than others in certain situations, these researchers concluded that an underhand throwing motion is less problematic. Objects thrown underhand on a slightly slower and curved path—rather than thrown over-hand on a faster and straight path—are easier to release and control.

According to this team's mathematical calculations, cricket bowlers who employ a rapid *underhand* motion, rather than an overhand motion, are more likely to strike the wicket. Basketball players who shoot foul shots *underhand*—compared to those who shoot them overhand—enjoy a marginal advantage. (Rick Barry made 90 percent of his underhand free throws during his fifteen-year NBA career.) To improve your accuracy, control, and power, throw the club underhand as rapidly as possible.

Releasing the club as you're moving toward the target requires some compensations. Therefore, right-handed golf-ers must release the club slightly *right* of target or toward right field and left-handed golfers slightly *left* of target or toward left field. It's easy to throw accurately when you're stationary and facing the target, but hard when you're turning.

Third, an underhand and rocking throwing motion enhances your *development*. Employing a natural and deliber-ate throwing motion—devoid of conscious controls—simpli-fies your swing, relaxes your hands and arms, flattens your lead wrist, rotates your hips, spins your wrist axles, plants your feet, shifts your weight, keeps the club on plane, and establishes a centrifugal path for your hands and club. Employing an under-hand and rocking throwing motion prevents you from over-rotating around your spine. To empower your release, move your trailing knee over your trailing big toe as fast as possible.

Fourth, throwing underhand and rocking your spine enhances your *follow-through*. In "Throwing Clubs Drill: When It's OK to Throw Clubs" published on the PGA's website, Mark Aumann writes, ". . . this [club-throwing] drill allows the player to get a better feel for the correct position at impact and follow through. That's critical because a study of six million people who have taken lessons through GolfTEC and their Tour player database shows a high degree of correlation between handicap and swing finish positions."

Reportedly, 90 percent of all golfers ignore their follow-through. The momentum derived from stepping, coiling, rocking, and free-wheeling your arms to throw the club over the front shoulder automatically produces a follow-through. To remind his pupils to follow through, Mike Austin would often say, "*Don't stop in Kansas City.*"

To perfect your follow-through, focus on your *trailing knee*. Turn it 30 degrees in your backswing; then turn it 120 degrees in your downswing and follow through. Ensure your trailing knee passes under your navel and points your belt buckle at the target. Your trailing knee and navel must keep turning.

Before you throw your Wombat 460cc driver—a.k.a. *The Goat Humper*—into your favorite water hazard, empty your mind. Wind up, fling it underhand, and watch it fly. When you learn to throw your clubs with reckless abandon at distant water hazards, trees, bunkers, and Porta Potties, your swing will improve significantly.

Consistency and Variability

Elite performers have set some amazing records. NBA star Michael Williams sank 97 consecutive foul shots. MLB pitcher Bartolo Colon threw 38 consecutive strikes. Champion dart-thrower Michael van Gerwen tossed 17 consecutive bulls-eyes. Bowler Tommy Gollick rolled 47 consecutive strikes. And PGA golfer Kevin Streelman carded 7 consecutive birdies. These are impressive streaks. However, why didn't their streaks keep going?

Stanford University research scientists Mark Churchland, Afsheen Afshar, and Krishna Shenoy came up with the answer. According to their findings, athletes are *unable* to repeat the same exact movement patterns again and again because the human brain plans every movement differently each time.

Every time your brain plans a physical movement to solve a particular problem—like driving a golf ball or shooting a foul shot—it does so anew each time. These pioneering researchers in their 2006 article titled "A Central Source of Movement Variability" published in *Neuron* admit that practice and training definitely assist the brain in solving problems effectively. However, the brains of humans and primates, unlike the processing capabilities of computers or machines, are not hard-wired for consistency. Simply stated, athletes improvise by default.

Researchers once believed that inconsistent or variable movement patterns were related to a phenomenon associated with one's muscles (i.e., "muscle memory"). However, research trials by Stanford University electrical engineers suggest that movement-variability or inconsistency flows from brain activity during the planning period.

The Stanford Team trained monkeys to perform simple reaching tasks. When the monkeys were shown a green spot, they were rewarded with juice when they reached out to touch it. When the monkeys were shown a red dot, however, they were trained to reach out rapidly.

These researchers then recorded and studied their brains' neural activity and arm speed. In thousands of trials, the researchers noted subtle variations in the monkeys' reaching movements. In sum, the monkeys varied their reaching movements consonant with slight neural variations in their brains' planning faculties.

Your brain cells alter their planning patterns for every movement. Therefore, every muscle-motor response—every golf swing, foul shot, or dart toss—is always slightly different. "Muscle memory" is a myth.

The lack of consistency is a frustrating problem among golfers. The brain, unable to plan every golf swing identically, is not built for *consistency*. It's built for *flexibility*. Given its ability to alter its planning mechanism differently for each movement, your brain can improvise to solve a vast number of unique problems and circumstances.

If you're hitting from a downhill lie, from heavy rough, from under a branch, or from the lip of a trap, your improvisational brain has the flexibility to swing accordingly. Since no two golf shots are exactly the same, you need consistency *and* flexibility.

Churchland states, "The nervous system was not designed to do the same thing over and over again. The nervous system was designed to be flexible. You typically find yourself doing things you've never done before."

Practice will help reduce variations in your swing and increase your consistency. However, practice can't change how your brain plans each swing anew. Analogously, a math student who has solved hundreds of quadratic equations will be better prepared to solve new quadratic equations compared to someone who's solved only two or three.

When you string together seven consecutive birdies during your next round, don't complain. Your brain is hard-wired for flexibility and consistency.

Mirror Neurons

Last Sunday you got teamed up with Vinnie. After Vinnie whiffed three times on the first tee, you averted your eyes. Vinnie, who likes to get his money's worth, doesn't mind high scores. Vinnie, who regrips his ball retriever once a season, loses approximately two dozen balls a round. When Vinnie gets in better shape, he plans to take up shuffleboard. Whenever you play with Vinnie, you're in shambles.

This week, however, you got paired up with Danny. When Danny smoked a 285-yard drive on the first hole, you were amazed. Danny, one of the best golfers at the club, has a fluid and effortless swing. Danny is always on the practice range perfecting his drives, long irons, and pitch shots. Most important, Danny is poised. If Danny had a heart attack on the course, he'd probably walk calmly to the ambulance and tell the EMTs not to rush on his account. Whenever you play with Danny, you thrive.

Neuroscientists who've recently discovered the existence of mirror neurons located in the frontal lobes of primates and humans can explain why your rounds with Vinnie and Danny differ greatly.

Mirror neurons and their role in *imitative learning* represent a major breakthrough. In fact, many researchers believe that mirror neurons will revolutionize cognitive science and psychology the way DNA has revolutionized biology and genetics.

Dr. Giacomo Rizzolatti, a neuroscientist at the University of Parma, accidentally discovered mirror neurons in 1996. To understand how primates plan and execute movements, he implanted thin computer wires into their brains. Then something amazing happened. When the monkeys observed Rizzolatti's assistant eating an ice cream cone, the computers started to bleep. Although the arms of the monkeys were motionless, the computer registered brain activity associated with arm-reaching movements.

In further experiments, Rizzolatti noticed that certain brain cells, now called mirror neurons, fired when the monkeys observed monkeys and humans eating peanuts, bananas, and raisins.

According to Rizzolatti, mirror neurons enable you to imitate and experience the movements of others. Being able to mimic someone's movements and read someone's intentions allows you to learn the complex and nuanced movements of expert golfers.

Mirror neurons, which induce imitative-movement patterns, explain why newborns reciprocate when you stick out your tongue, why you yawn when others yawn, and why you laugh when others laugh. These imitative responses are examples of subconscious and involuntary actions based on neural mechanisms. It's as if your brain were equipped with a neurological simulator capable of imitating and understanding selected behaviors.

When Bobby Jones was seven, soon after his family moved next door to East Lake Golf Course, he studied and imitated the swing of head professional Stewart Maiden. Bobby Jones claimed that his observations of Maiden's swing were the only "lessons" he ever received. Using his mirror neurons to imitate Maiden's swing, Bobby Jones created a foundation for his own legendary swing.

Legendary Lessons (2016), edited by Claudia Mazzucco, explores the thoughts and practices of Walter Hagen. In an enlightening chapter titled "How to Develop the Imitative Faculty," Roger and Joyce Wetherel discuss Hagen's theory of learning swing mechanics. Hagen, who obviously knew nothing about mirror neurons, believed that your imitative mind is most active between the ages of 12 and 20.

Hagen insisted that novices should mimic the rhythm, grip, stance, and movements of their golfing idols. Although novices must play their own shots, they should imagine themselves reproducing the expert strokes of others. By faithfully imitating the swings of expert golfers, you will acquire a similar style. Through osmosis you'll develop your own expert swing.

As your brain plans and executes the swinging motion, it engages 86 billion brain cells. However, mirror neurons are special brain cells. Mirror neurons fire not only when you plan and execute your own movements, but also when you observe the movements of others.

Neuroscientist Dr. Vittorio Gallese states, "This neural mechanism is involuntary and automatic . . . we don't have to *think* about what other people are doing or feeling, we simply *know*."

Dr. Marco Iacoboni, a noted UCLA neurobiologist, in an interview published in *UCLA Magazine* discusses the link between mirror neurons and learning athletic skills. He claims you learn athletic skills in two ways: (1) through *direct* experience or participation and (2) through *indirect* experience or observation. For example, when you observe golf on television, your mirror neurons start firing. When that occurs, you golf vicariously. Dr. Iacoboni claims that mirror neurons work best when you view live rather than videotaped behaviors.

Sports psychologists who've studied dart-throwing, juggling, dancing, and other skills maintain that *indirect* experience improves certain skill sets. In a recent study, researchers compared 32 participatory golfers who rolled putts *and* 32 golfers who simply held a putter, observed others, and mimicked practice strokes. Exposed to the same instructional protocols, both groups of golfers of similar proficiency improved *equally!*

To enhance your skill sets, integrate direct and indirect experience, performance and observation, cognitive thought, and sensory stimulation. Integrate—don't separate. The mirror neurons of experienced and knowledgeable golfers, compared to those of novices, reap the greatest rewards. Therefore, do your homework. Mirror neurons will reduce the ordeal of learning swing mechanics.

Noted neuroscientist Dr. Vilayanur S. Ramachandran posits that mirror neurons sharpen your powers of *self-awareness*. In other words, mirror neurons turn not only *outward* to imitate the movement of others, but also turn *inward* to self-monitor your own movements. According to Dr. Ramachandran, mirror neurons induce the sensation that someone, perhaps your instructor, is monitoring your performance.

Don't confuse *visualizing* with *imitating*. These are different cognitive modes. Visualization, which occurs in the occipital lobe located at the back of your head, involves the creation and repetition of imaginative mental images designed to boost self-confidence and ensure success. Visualization stretches the limits of your imagination and instills positive thoughts for growth.

When you visualize your tee shot soaring like a rocket down the fairway, for example, you are willing it to happen. You've hit long and straight drives before; therefore, why not this time, too? Visualizations provide creative and sensory analogues to simplify and clarify complex thoughts.

Imitating, however, denotes the subconscious duplication of movement patterns observed in others. Imitation employs selected mirror neurons. By mimicking actual movement patterns, you can acquire and understand how others move. According to neuroscientists, the emerging field of imitative learning represents a major breakthrough in cognitive theory.

Your mirror neurons allow you to learn new things and remain cognitively fit as you age. "Neuroplasticity" denotes the brain's capacity to process, adapt, and organize new information. Cognitively fit old dogs can learn new tricks. P.G. Wodehouse, the British humorist, wrote until he was 93. Abraham Goldstein, former Yale Law School Dean, tutored students until he was 103. When you're cognitively fit, working is more fun than having fun.

Therefore, project your mirror neurons *outwardly* to observe the expert swings of others *and* project them *inwardly* to monitor your own swing. When you vicariously enter the bodies of expert players, you swing by proxy. If imitative learning worked for Bobby Jones and Walter Hagen, it can work for you.

Sam Snead defeated Ben Hogan in an 18-hole playoff to win The Masters in 1954. Snead claimed it was the most memorable and cherished round of his career. During his many rounds with Hogan, Snead—to avoid subconscious and involuntary imitation—claimed he never once watched Hogan swing. Sam Snead may have anticipated something about mirror neurons.

Learned Helplessness

When an American tourist in India observed a massive elephant tethered to an iron stake with a small rope, she asked the mahout, "How can such a small rope prevent a powerful elephant from wandering away?" The mahout replied, "Elephants are conditioned to remain docile. Soon after an elephant is born, we attach a small rope around its front foot to restrain it. As the elephant matures, it continues to believe that it can't free itself. Thus, we rarely have to use chains, cables, or shackles."

Like docile elephants, stymied golfers tend to remain stuck. Conditioned by protracted failure, many golfers seem unwilling and unable to rid their bad habits, challenge their beliefs, and revolutionize their thinking. Many failed golfers, like tethered elephants, are trussed to defunct principles, practices, and methodologies.

An elephant constrained by a small rope illustrates a phenomenon that social scientists call "learned helplessness," a condition whereby animals and humans remain permanently vulnerable. Learned helplessness is synonymous with stagnation.

In 1967, Martin Seligman, a University of Pennsylvania psychologist, developed his theory of learned helplessness by experimenting on dogs. In his experiment, Seligman sub-jected three groups of dogs to mild electric shocks. The proac-tive dogs in Groups 1 and 2 learned to activate levers to con-trol their shocks. However, the dogs in Group 3—subjected to random, uncontrolled, and inescapable shocks—developed "learned helplessness."

Following the conditioning phase of his experiment, Seligman placed the same three groups of dogs in a box con-taining a small partition that dogs could easily jump over to escape being shocked. The dogs in Groups 1 and 2, condi-tioned to escape the shocks, readily jumped over the partition. However, the dogs in Group 3—conditioned by learned help-lessness—simply lay down, whined, and accepted the shocks.

Despite Seligman's rewards, threats, and exhortations for the dogs in Group 3 to jump over the partition, they continued to endure the shocks. Twice Seligman had to pick up the dogs' legs and reposition their bodies before they willfully jumped over the electrified grid. To overcome their learned helpless-ness, these dogs had to be physically lifted over the barrier.

Is that what you need to improve your swing? To trigger your improvement, does someone have to lift you over the "electri-fied grid of failure" to reverse your learned helplessness?

When it comes to learned helplessness, golfers are not alone. Remedial learners, abused spouses, bullied students, welfare recipients, sick patients, and jobless workers are often victims of learned helplessness.

Consider swapping *learned helplessness* for *learned optimism*. If you have an imaginary rope tied around your front foot, you'll never break free. You'll never grow. Without growth, you might as well be dead.

Unlearning

Several years ago, Don Trahan—a noted PGA Professional, innovative thinker, and founder of Peak Performance Golf— asked me a provocative question: "Must golfers *unlearn* bad habits to *learn* good ones?"

To understand *unlearning* from a neurological perspective, let's first examine *learning*. In their book *Neuroscience for Leadership* (2015), Tara Swart, Kitty Chisholm, and Paul Brown claim that learning denotes enhancing the brain's capacity to connect tiny pulses of electricity between the synapses or small gaps separating the brain's 86 billion neurons.

To imagine how your brain functions, hold your two fists close together without touching. One fist represents the axon of one neuron. The other fist represents the dendrite of another neuron. The gap between represents the synapse. The axon of one neuron releases a chemical or neurotransmitter that binds and connects with dendrites of other neurons. Each of your 86 billion neurons make as many as 10,000 synaptic connections. In a matter of milliseconds, your brain can make trillions of electrical connections.

In his TED Talk, "I am My Connectomes," physicist Sebastian Seung calls your brain's genetic pattern of electrical connections a *connectome*. Seung compares your brain's flow of electrical impulses to a stream in a forest. Your stream of neurons never sits still. However, your *connectome*—the streambed formed over time—guides and reshapes the flow of water. Seung states, "Neural activity is the stream and the connectome is its bed." Simply put, the neural *flow* of your golf swing keeps changing as the neural *streambed* of your golf swing keeps deepening.

During your lifetime, your stream of neurons will erode its banks, flow over rocks, and form small eddies. Your flowing stream of electrical impulses keeps changing the configuration of your neural network.

When you learn something new, your neurons require a greater electrical charge to bridge the synaptic gap. As these electrical charges cross the synaptic gap with greater frequency, the easier learning becomes. Simply put, first-time learning is always exhausting and demanding.

Youngsters with unformed brains have considerable flexibility and plasticity. That's why kids learn so quickly. In her online interview with *Fast Company*, Dr. Deborah Ancona states, "It turns out that we, as human beings, develop neural pathways, and the more we use those neural pathways over years and years and years, they become very stuck and deeply embedded, moving into deeper portions of the brain. By the time we get to the age of 25, we just have so many existing pathways that our brain relies on; it's hard to break free of them."

Admittedly, you'll never learn and change as quickly and easily as you did during childhood. However, neuroplasticity—the brain's ability to create new brain cells and form new neural pathways—allows you to learn new skills and adopt new behaviors.

Researchers Judah Pollack and Olivia Fox Cabane liken the brain to a flower garden requiring occasional pruning. Unlearning involves breaking down old neural connections.

These researchers call the unlearning process "synaptic pruning."

On Fast Company's website, Pollack and Cabane published a fascinating article titled "Your Brain's Delete Button And How to Use It." Pollack and Cabane state: "Imagine your brain is a garden, except instead of growing flowers, fruits, and vegetables, you grow synaptic connections between neurons. . . . *Glial cells* are the gardeners of your brain; they act to speed up signals between certain neurons. But other glial cells are the waste removers, pulling up weeds, killing pests, and raking up dead leaves. Your brain's pruning gardeners are called *microglial cells*. They prune your synaptic connections."

Neuroscientists claim that the brain uses *existing* neural pathways to create *new* ones. Your existing pathways make it easier and quicker to build new pathways and learn new things. Neurons overwrite—but never erase—old neural pathways.

The learning process is analogous to growth rings in a tree trunk. When you learn something new, another ring grows over an existing ring. With every passing year, trees add a new ring on top of the previous ring. New growth rings overlap—but do not destroy or erase—old growth rings.

Why do so many golfers refuse to change their failed thinking? Psychologists and economists often attribute illogical thinking and failed learning to "The Fallacy of Sunk Costs." A sunk cost is a previous investment of money, time, effort, or emotion that cannot be recovered. For example, suppose you invested considerable time, money, and effort developing your swing before you identified your biggest swing flaw: overrotating your hips. To stop overrotating your hips, you must accept your sunk costs. This isn't easy. Your brain protects old learning that took years to acquire and resists the creation of new neural pathways and fresh memory traces.

Pruning your garden, uncluttering your mental attic, and replacing old neural connections take effort. Seneca wrote,

"The mind is slow in unlearning what it has been long in learning." Unlearning is twice as hard as learning.

How do you *unlearn* destructive swing habits? Mark Bonchek, in "Why the Problem with Learning is Unlearning" published in the *Harvard Business Review*, offers three suggestions on unlearning: recognize your bad habits, adopt new models, and refresh your learning.

First, recognize that your old habits are irrelevant and ineffective. This is a daunting task because you're probably unaware of your flawed thinking and doing. You're accustomed to thinking and doing the wrong things for so long that you ignore them. Moreover, you've invested considerable time, energy, and ego into your errant ways. Why would you want to start over? Unlearning involves fighting against inertia. Before you can fix a bad habit, like coming over the top, you first must recognize it. Therefore, videotape, monitor, and analyze your swing.

To learn, unlearn, and relearn a proper swing, you must obtain clear and accurate information to deconstruct it piece by piece. For example, if you want to learn the proper impact position, you must know what the proper impact position is and how to attain it.

To unlearn and relearn the proper impact position, for example, requires approximately 100 proper repetitions to create a new neural pathway and many hundred more repetitions to create default pathways.

Since your brain doesn't know what to unlearn, your mind must tell it. What should most golfers unlearn first? Start by unlearning *the hit impulse*. Make this your initial unlearning goal.

The hit impulse—a natural, involuntary, and destructive urge—invites you to overswing. To unlearn the hit impulse, focus on *swinging* the club through the impact area using centrifugal force and inertia. Don't focus on *hitting* the ball using brute muscular force.

In *The Natural Golf Swing* (1988), George Knudson, the famed Canadian PGA Professional, wrote: "Maybe you visualized a full swing, maybe you thought only of swinging through to your target. Or maybe you didn't think anything. The point is *you gave up control and the result was that you gained control.* You stopped thinking about what to do with the club and let it flow on its own. The club went along on a pure path and you went along for the ride. You let centrifugal force and inertia work."

However, a *natural* swing as Knudson describes is completely *unnatural* given the fact that humans have been striking objects with brute force for over 200,000 years. For golfers to unlearn the timeless, natural, and primal impulse of using their muscles to bludgeon objects is a daunting task. Unlearning the hit impulse may be a golfer's greatest challenge.

To unlearn the hit impulse, make every swing a *practice swing.* In your practice swing, when you're not ball-bound, your arms are light, hands are soft, and wrists are flexible. In your practice swing, you're patient, composed, carefree, and relaxed.

Build new neural pathways and superimpose new growth rings in your brain's tree trunk. Stop rushing and grabbing. Empty your mind. In a smooth and rhythmic practice swing, your main objective is to swish the clubhead through the impact area. There's plenty of room on a fifty-yard-wide fairway to accommodate your two-inch diameter ball.

If the hit impulse—or any other swing flaw—escapes your awareness, you can't unlearn it. Do you recall what happened to Ebenezer Scrooge? He was a miserable curmudgeon before he saw things clearly and changed his ways. Charles Dickens nailed it. Resolve to see things clearly and unlearn your bad habits.

Second, find a new model or paradigm to achieve your goals. Don't view new ways through the lens of the past. Don't become a prisoner of previous thoughts and behaviors by confirming your existing beliefs. Refresh your thinking and learning. To exceed the norm, you must break the norm.

Within the disorder of your game—your poor drives, pitches, chips, and putts—valuable lessons reside. Use your brain, YouTube, and Google to replace your failed beliefs, methods, and habits. When I became a contrarian, I reversed my thinking and improved my game.

Third, adopt new learning habits. Learn how to learn. Employ integrative thinking by merging opposites. Resist the tendency to fall back into your old ways. Create triggers or reminders that you're a different person and you're doing things differently. Since your cognitive bandwidth is limited, ensure that what you're unlearning warrants your time and energy.

To unlearn effectively, you need ample mental focus and energy. To unlearn, your brain needs more oxygenated blood. Since unlearning is exhausting work, be selective in your focus.

Learning something *new* does not necessarily mean that you've successfully unlearned something *old*. The fact that you can finally hit seven long and straight drives for every ten doesn't evidence permanent learning, unlearning, and relearning. It simply evidences that you possess the requisite willpower, focus, and potential to transform yourself. However, willpower and focus are finite assets.

In his book *Your Brain at Work*, David Rock tells you to attach a specific name to the practice or habit you're trying to unlearn. Naming the thing you're trying to unlearn will narrow your focus.

Elkhonon Goldberg, author of *The New Executive Brain*, asserts that your conscious mind, located in the prefrontal cortex, is your brain's orchestra leader that controls decision making and selected behavior. Naming what you want to unlearn, therefore, activates your prefrontal cortex, enhances focus, and stimulates visualizations.

Must you unlearn old knowledge and habits before you can relearn new knowledge and habits? The answer is no. Knowing the flaws in your swing is as important as knowing how to fix them. You don't have to unlearn your inefficient swing to relearn an efficient swing. To improve your swing, you must build new neural pathways over old neural pathways.

Unlearning and relearning are based on previous knowledge and existing neural pathways. Unlearning will not eliminate your lousy swing. However, unlearning makes inefficient swings less available and efficient swings more available.

Your game—using nerve cells and circuits as building blocks—has developed over time. William James called this "your private self." Changing neural pathways that took years to create is difficult. To change your swing, curb your rigid responses and become more flexible.

To actualize learning, unlearning, and relearning, you need new and better information. Alvin Toffler, in *Rethinking the Future*, wrote, "The illiterate of the 21st century will not be those who cannot read and write, but those who cannot learn, unlearn, and relearn."

Robin Hood

COVID-19—responsible for infecting and killing millions of people in 212 nations and territories—has reached pandemic proportions. Researchers say that 50 percent of the people with COVID-19 are unaware they have it. One's unawareness of having a contagious disease allows it to spread throughout the world.

One's unawareness of having a contagious swing flaw also allows it to spread throughout the world. *Initiating the downswing with your torso instead of your hands and arms*—the coronavirus of the golf swing—has reached pandemic proportions. The most important split second in the swing—when everything must be sanitized and sterile—occurs at the start of your downswing. Let me explain.

Imagine the golf swing as an anatomical horse race. The outside horse, which has a longer distance to travel and must accelerate to catch up with the inside horse on the rail, represents your hands. The inside horse represents your torso and shoulders. Unless you accelerate your hands, which must travel a longer distance, they will never catch up with your torso.

The ability to blend different actions that are operating at different speeds—namely, the swinging of your arms and the turning motion of your body—is the hallmark of expert golfers.

Inexpert golfers initiate their downswing with the slow muscles of their torso and shoulders perhaps because they're overly concerned about "staying connected." However, if you initiate your downswing with your torso and/or shoulders, you'll approach the ball on too steep a plane.

"Loading" refers to the way golfers use their hands and wrists at the start of the downswing to create a 90-degree angle or lag between their leading arm and the shaft. When you initiate the downswing with your hands, you're actually *transferring*—not *loading*—energy from your hands to the club. Loading is akin to snapping a whip.

In *The Golfing Machine*, Homer Kelley discusses different types of loading, including *drive loading* and *drag loading*. In drive loading, you grab the handle with both hands as if you were swinging an axe—à la Paul Bunyan—from the side. Conversely, in drag loading, you grab the handle with your dominant hand—à la Robin Hood—as if you were removing an arrow from a quiver to load a long bow.

Ben Hogan famously compared using his hands to initiate his downswing to removing an arrow from a quiver slung over his right shoulder.

In his description of drag loading, Homer Kelley writes: "Start the club down as though it were being drawn from a quiver like an arrow—feather-end first. Maintain this motion until the release switches end. Centrifugal force will set in when the clubhead passes to the outside arc of the hands and will begin to pull into its own incidental orbit."

To drag load, move your hands and arms *out* and *away* from your body. This movement—a critical component in your swing's complex system—creates space for your trailing elbow to move inside your trailing hip and generate power. No swing component exists in isolation.

Many golfers wrongly confuse drag loading with casting. Drag loading may feel like casting; however, it's not. Drag loading occurs when you're turning. Casting occurs when you stop turning.

To drag load, imagine at address that your nose is facing 12 o'clock. Next, bring the club to the top, counterrotate your trailing upper arm, then turn your torso to face the 2 o'clock position. Next, pretend you're Robin Hood. Grab the feather-end of the arrow, remove it from your quiver, stretch out your lead arm, reduce the bend in your trailing elbow to 45 degrees, hinge your wrists to invert the shaft, then load your bow. This is how your hands, wrists, and arms drag load.

When you initiate your downswing à la Robin Hood, reduce your lag angle—formed between your lead forearm and the shaft—to 45 degrees. Simply throw the clubhead at the ball as if you're removing the shaft of an arrow from its quiver. This action releases lag and aligns the shaft with your lead arm to form a straight line. Always straighten your trailing arm and elbow after impact, never before.

Experts golfers subconsciously *release* lag and initiate their downswing with their hands and arms. Poor golfers consciously *hold* lag and initiate their downswing with their torso.

Choking under Pressure

During The Open in 1999, Jean Van de Velde made dubious golf history. Standing on the tee of the finishing hole—a 449-yard par four—Van de Velde held a three-stroke lead. He needed only a double bogey to become the first golfer from France since Arnaud Massey in 1907 to win The Open. Unfortunately, Van de Velde choked under pressure. Since then "Jean Van de Velde" and "choke artist" have become synonymous terms.

Hitting driver, Van de Velde sliced his ball over the Barry Burn—a winding lateral water hazard—onto the 17th fairway. Instead of laying up with his second shot, he went for the green with a 2-iron. His ball struck the railing of the grandstand, bounced back 50 yards, and landed in heavy rough. Playing his third shot from knee-high grass, Van de Velde hit his ball into another lateral water hazard.

Planning to play his partially submerged ball, Van de Velde rolled up his pants and removed his shoes and socks. Thinking better of it, however, he took a penalty drop and hit his fifth shot into a greenside bunker. Mercifully, Van de Velde blasted out of the bunker to within eight feet and one-putted for a triple bogey 7. He finished in a tie with Paul Lawrie and

Justin Leonard. Paul Lawrie won the four-hole playoff and took home The Claret Jug.

Neuroscientists theorize why athletes choke under pressure and how to alleviate it. Let's start with the basics. You have two nervous systems: a *central nervous system* (CNS) in your brain and spinal cord and a *peripheral nervous system* (PNS) in your hands, arms, skin, and other areas. These nervous systems are comprised of neurons that communicate with one another by secreting trace chemicals and emitting tiny electrical charges.

Muscle movement messages—akin to orders from a general—flow *downward* from the CNS. Sensation messages—like responses from the troops—flow *upward* from the PNS. Millions of neurons in both nervous systems exchange messages related to movement and sensations.

When you first learn a skill, your neural-motor pathways—subjected to considerable "neural noise" or distractions—are initially slow and weak. With considerable practice and myelination (i.e., the buildup of fatty insulation), your neural-motor pathways become stronger, faster, and less susceptible to neural noise.

In learning complex skills, each stage (i.e., the *cognitive, associative,* and *autonomous*) requires a specific focus. In the *cognitive* or beginner phase, you employ *internal* focus or conscious cues to break down and mechanically execute complex movements. In the *associative* or intermediate phase, when your movements become more fluid and consistent, you merge *internal* and *external* focus (i.e., conscious and subconscious cues) to execute complex movements. In the *autonomous* or expert phase, after years of deliberate practice, you employ *external* focus or subconscious cues to perform consistently, intuitively, and autonomously.

Choking occurs when expert athletes, despite having practiced complex movements thousands of times, revert to *internal* focus under stressful situations. Expert athletes performing well-rehearsed movement patterns choke under pressure when "neural noise" blocks their subconscious, natural, or autonomous movement patterns.

Neuroscientists offer two overlapping theories to explain the choking phenomenon: *The Over-Arousal Theory* and *The Self-Monitoring Theory.* Both theories postulate that stress impairs the prefrontal cortex where *executive functioning* and *working memory* reside.

The Over-Arousal Theory posits that excessive arousal in the form of high rewards, emotional distraction, social pressure, and loss aversion induces choking. Psychologists Robert Yerkes and John Dodson in 1908 established an empirical relationship between arousal and performance. The Yerkes–Dodson Law, graphically depicted in a bell curve, postulates that performance levels vary depending on the amount of physiological and mental stress involved. In brief, arousal levels that are either too high or too low impair performance.

Lower arousal levels are more appropriate for intellectually demanding tasks (e.g., taking exams). Higher arousal levels are more appropriate for physical tasks demanding stamina and persistence (e.g., running marathons). Arousal levels in expert performers must be just right.

Extreme loss aversion and intense motivation during high-stakes competition also induce choking. Choking frequently occurs when accomplished athletes experience what psychologists call "a stereotypical threat" (i.e., the need to perform well in public and live up to perceived expectations). Overarousal inhibits the prefrontal cortex by activating the brain's reward pathway by releasing large amounts of *dopamine.*

In "The Functions of Dopamine and How Does it Affect You?" Radiyyah Hussein states that dopamine, a chemical messenger in the brain, sends information from one neuron to another. He writes, "The main structure in your brain that controls all sorts of bodily movements is the basal ganglia. In order for your basal ganglia to function at peak efficiency, it relies on the secretion of a specific amount of dopamine from neighboring neurons. . . . However, if the basal ganglia receives too much dopamine, it will cause your body to make unnecessary movements."

Simply stated, overarousal releases excessive amounts of dopamine that prevent your muscles from performing complex skills.

The Self-Monitoring Theory posits that excessive internal focus or overthinking induces choking among expert athletes. Dr. Sian Beilock—a neuroscientist, psychologist, kinesiologist and author of *Choke* (2011)—has used MRI equipment and neuroimaging to examine the brains of skilled athletes, especially golfers, in stressful situations.

Beilock states, "It is not the pressure in a pressure situation that distracts us into performing poorly. The pressure makes us worry and want to control our actions too much. And you cannot think your way through a routine, practiced action, like making a 3-foot putt."

Golfers who choke under pressure mistakenly *increase*—rather than *decrease*—their thinking. Since their brain got them into trouble in the first place, they wrongly assume their brain can extricate them from trouble.

The Self-Monitoring Theory holds that analyzing your own complex movements (i.e., internal focus) disrupts your ability to function intuitively and automatically. Dr. Gabrielle Wulf's "Constrained Action Hypothesis" asserts that athletes who excessively monitor their *actions* produce inelegant, mechanical, and inflexible movements. Conversely, athletes who monitor the *consequences of their actions* (i.e., external focus) perform skillfully, reliably, and fluidly.

Overthinking—*paralysis by analysis*—induces choking among athletes under duress. Beilock states, "When outside stresses shift attention, the *prefrontal cortex* stops working the way it should. We focus on aspects of what we are doing that should be out of consciousness." Skilled athletes who excel under duress use streamlined brain circuitry that bypasses the prefrontal cortex. Why is this important?

Executive functioning takes place in the prefrontal cortex located in the frontal lobe. Executive functioning, a complex cognitive mechanism, manages reason, logic, problem solving, planning, and memory. In her article "Executive Functions," Adele Diamond writes, "Executive functions make possible mentally playing with ideas; taking the time to think before acting; meeting novel, unanticipated challenges; resisting temptations; and staying focused."

Executive functioning plays a significant role in working memory, thinking outside the box, adapting quickly to changing circumstances, seeing things from different perspectives, and achieving goals.

Van de Velde's disastrous meltdown—flowing from impulsive decisions, faulty reasoning, overthinking, and memory lapses—illustrates how stress affects the prefrontal cortex and impairs executive functioning. A deficit in his executive functioning helps explain why Van de Velde mistakenly believed he had a two-stroke (not a three-stroke) lead on the final hole.

In her Human Performance Lab lined with artificial turf, Beilock asked LPGA golfers to putt on a makeshift green for monetary rewards before an evaluative audience. Her subjects were 20 percent less accurate compared to previous tests when attempting putts between three and five feet. "Golfers often choke when they think too much. Skilled athletes use streamlined brain circuitry that largely bypasses the prefrontal cortex, the seat of awareness. When outside stresses shift attention, the prefrontal cortex stops working the way it should. We focus on aspects of what we are doing that should be out of our consciousness."

In another study, Beilock asked inexperienced and experienced LPGA subjects, hooked up to MRI technology, to hit shots to a flagstick 100 yards away. Neuroimaging clearly indicated that the brain areas associated with fear and anxiety were more active among less experienced players. Conversely, the brain areas of more experienced players—who learned to "enter the zone" and "quiet their minds"—exhibited considerably less fear and anxiety.

Dr. Beilock offers golfers several key suggestions to alleviate choking when they're putting:

1. Be quick on the greens—not hurried, but not overly deliberate. "It helps to have a routine, but putting as quickly as was reasonable is a good idea. We told people to err on the side of being quick, and it worked."
2. Find something to focus on, like the manufacturer's name or logo on the ball. It can help prevent the prefrontal cortex from regulating your movements too closely.
3. Employ a brief mantra. When you're putting, use a word like "*smooth*" or a three-word timing device like "*back-and-through.*"
4. Change something in your grip, setup, stance, etc., to reprogram your neural pathways and improve your execution. Recently, I changed the shaft angle of my putter by toeing rather than heeling the putter head. When I toed the putter, thereby setting the shaft in a more vertical or upright position, I stopped worrying about opening and closing the putter face. I kept the putter face square to the target. Under pressure, straight lines make putting easier and better.
5. Focus on your goal and target—not your mechanics. Some people look at the hole rather than the ball or visualize the back of the cup. Beilock claims, "It sends a signal to the brain to achieve a certain outcome."

6. Learn to handle pressure. Beilock states, "It happens very subtly, but understanding how your body is going to feel under pressure and learning to handle it is a skill in itself." When you're putting with others, play games for small stakes. When you're putting alone, create personal incentives (e.g., making 3 ten-footers before leaving).

Jean Van de Velde isn't alone. During the 1946 Masters, Ben Hogan lined up a two-foot putt on the final hole and missed the cup entirely. He lost by a stroke to Herman Keiser. During the 1983 Open, Hale Irwin, on the final hole after nearly sinking a 20-footer, whiffed when he nonchalantly attempted his tap-in and lost by a stroke to Tom Watson. During the opening hole of the 2016 Masters, Ernie Els missed seven consecutive putts—including five tap-ins—and carded a ten.

Nonathletes also choke. You choked when you botched the champagne toast at Fat Tony's wedding. You also choked when you made three costly errors at second base during the final inning of the Rotary Club softball game last summer.

Weighted Clubs

To loosen up before a round, you swing two or three clubs. When you played baseball and softball, you warmed up with a weighted bat. Why should golf be any different? In baseball and golf, you use the same muscles to perform the same movements. Therefore, why warm up differently?

Expert golfers rarely warm up by slowly swinging several clubs. Most seasoned pros warm up by rapidly swinging the inverted shaft of their drivers to make loud swooshing sounds. Apparently, professionals know something you don't.

Exercise scientists see advantages and disadvantages in swinging weighted clubs. Dr. Michael Voight, a Belmont University clinical therapist and member of Titleist's Advisory Board, claims that amateur golfers with limited hip and back flexibility benefit by warming up using relatively heavy objects. Conversely, expert golfers with excellent flexibility benefit by warming up with relatively light objects. Voight recommends that all golfers, regardless of their flexibility, should swing both right-handed and left-handed to improve their coordination and balance.

To increase bat speed, professional baseball players routinely warm up in the batter's box by swinging weighted bats and lead pipes. After swinging a weighted bat, you can swing a normal bat much quicker. However, a recent study suggests that warming up with a weighted bat or club is counterproductive. This is an important finding.

Steven Zinder, research scientist at UNC, claims that swinging a heavier bat significantly slows down your bat head speed and reduces your power. In his article published in the *Journal of Strength and Conditioning Research*, Zinder writes, "Swinging *light* or normal weight lumber just before stepping up to the plate helps players become accustomed to swinging fast . . . repetition is key to athletic training . . ."

Swinging a heavy object seems to make sense biomechanically. However, Zinder claims, "If you want to swing faster, you need to practice by swinging faster." Warming up with a lighter club will train your muscles to swing faster. Warming up with a heavier club will train your muscles to swing slower. Moreover, a baseball swing relies on gross motor movements for raw power. A golf swing relies on fine motor movements for supple quickness.

Dr. Mel Siff, a respected sports scientist, claimed that warming up with a weighted club changes the mechanical recruitment of muscles and alters your club path. In sum, when you swing a weighted club you alter your brain's swing engram (i.e., memory trace), and thereby you swing differently. You want your practice swing to duplicate, not distort, the path, timing, and speed of your normal swing.

Your muscles contain both slow-twitch and fast-twitch fibers. Slow-twitch fibers, which fatigue slowly, provide runners, swimmers, and cyclists with endurance. Fast-twitch fibers, which fatigue quickly, provide golfers, sprinters, and baseball pitchers with short bursts of energy. In the downswing, your fast-twitch fibers must fire rapidly to generate power and distance.

To improve your ball-striking and increase clubhead speed, warm up by swinging light objects at high speed. To strengthen your core muscles, however, use a medicine ball or kettle weights. Such exercise routines will strengthen your rotational power without interfering with your golf swing.

Golfers and Dieters

Golfers and dieters—failure-prone and adrift in a vast sea of dubious advice—are in the same metaphorical boat. Definitive studies, indisputable proof, conclusive findings, lengthy trials, and scientific research have yet to determine which golf methodology or dietary plan works best. If one golf or dietary program proved superior, inferior programs would vanish.

Golfers and dieters—exposed to a myriad of contradictory regimens—need to examine the cold facts. There's no such thing as a universal or optimum golf methodology or diet.

In the absence of conclusive evidence, golfers and dieters must sift through anecdotal evidence, unsupported claims, glowing testimonials, cherry-picked statistics, nonrepresentative samples, unscientific proof, commercial promotions, and cognitive biases.

William Banting, a London undertaker, introduced and popularized the low-carb diet in 1863. Today, researchers still don't know if this or any diet works best. At the 2018 international symposium of The Obesity Society, leading scientists presented contradictory findings on high-profile diets.

In his 2018 presentation, Dr. Christopher Gardner reported that his Stanford Medical School study was inconclusive. Dr. Gardner separated 619 subjects into two groups whose members received equal amounts of low-fat and low-carb calories for one year. The average weight loss among all subjects was 13 pounds. However, some subjects lost 60 pounds and others gained 20 pounds. Neither diet proved superior.

According to Gardner, low-fat and low-carb dieters lose weight in the same proportion regardless of their insulin levels or genetics. Low-fat diets work better for some, and low-carb diets work better for others.

Gardner asserts that successful dieters must (1) make healthy and informed choices such as consuming fewer processed foods, less sugar, and more fresh fruits and vegetables and (2) change their relationship with food: "It's because we're all very different and we're just starting to understand the reasons for this diversity. Maybe we shouldn't be asking what's the best diet, but what's the best diet for whom?"

To customize your thinking and learning, ask yourself, *"What's the best golf methodology for me?"*

Some diets and golf regimens work better than others. No specific diet or golf regimen works best for everyone. I'm not saying that certain methodologies haven't benefited some golfers. I'm saying that no methodology has benefited all golfers. Diets and golf are person-specific.

Dr. Eric Topol, cardiologist, recently conducted a study involving over 1,000 patients. When he used artificial intelligence to analyze 1.5 million glucose measurements to create a personalized diet algorithm, he made an astounding discovery—that food intake is not the key determinant in losing or gaining weight. The key dietary determinant is the bacterial content in the gut.

Dr. Topol states, ". . . we have learned how simplistic and naïve the assumption of a universal diet is. It is both biologically and physiologically implausible. It contradicts the remarkable heterogeneity of human metabolism. . . . A good diet, it turns out, has to be individualized . . . there is no such thing as a universal diet."

Despite decades of research into dieting and golf, it's surprising how little we know about both. Dismal golf and dietary outcomes—predicated on naive and simplistic assumptions—are surprisingly similar.

Moreover, short-term dietary and golf regimens that promise lasting results simply don't work. Long-term success for golfers and dieters demands constant vigilance, motivation, and focus.

To demonstrate the movement patterns of expert golfers, instructors often show pupils swing videos of Ben Hogan, Jack Nicklaus, Mickey Wright, or Adam Scott. However, if a Tour Pro doesn't share your parameters—including gender, age, height, build, fitness level, athleticism, muscularity, flexibility, range of motion, forearm length, upper arm length, trunk length, rhythm, balance, timing, hand-eye coordination, reflexes, suppleness, athleticism, and natural ability—what's the point?

If you're obese and arthritic, you can't swing like Justin Rose. All golf methodologies are person-specific. Hence you must customize, personalize, and individualize your thinking and learning.

Suggesting that one methodology will suit all golfers is insane. To develop a single methodology, one must closely assess many different protocols and monitor thousands of golfers with varied backgrounds, aptitudes, learning styles, and motivation levels.

Viable and accelerated methodologies do exist for learning and teaching guitar, dance, memory retention, speed-reading, etc. Karate pupils exposed to standardized and uniform kicking, blocking, and punching techniques improve dramatically.

Conversely, golf pupils exposed to varied body and club positions—based on an instructional biases, personal preferences, and subjective practices—improve marginally.

Becoming your own golf guru involves several steps. *First, recognize that your existing methodology doesn't work.* Old mental models and long-term habits are difficult to break. Admittedly, learning new models and starting over will be tedious. However, why settle for something that doesn't work?

Second, replace your defunct methodology with something better. Your brain, given its unlimited capacity, can hold one quadrillion bits of information during your lifetime. Unfortunately, your mind—given its finite capacity and limited time to learn—can pay attention to only a few things at once. Since old information and long-term memories harden as you age, replacing a defunct methodology demands patience, reason, and imagination. Select a viable teaching and learning regimen that suits you.

Third, engrain new mental habits. To engrain and remember new golf habits, employ mental triggers. For example, to mentally engrain my new setup habits, I devised my *G-P-S Trigger*. At setup, this mental trigger consciously alerts me to use my new, multifaceted *grip, posture,* and *stance.* Without mental triggers, you'll revert to your old habits.

Models

In 1963, True Temper commissioned George Manning, a mechanical engineer, to design and build an electromechanical robot to test golf equipment for the USGA. Manning, using high-speed photography, analyzed the swings of countless professional and amateur golfers. Manning concluded that Byron Nelson's swing was so efficient and consistent that only a machine could duplicate it. Accordingly, Manning built his robot based on Nelson's swing.

When steel shafts were starting to replace hickory shafts in the early 1930s, Nelson modified his swing to accommodate this transition. In 1945 alone, the year Nelson retired at age 34, he had won 18 tournaments (including 11 in a row) and set the annual scoring record by averaging 68.33 strokes per round.

Considered "The Father of the Modern Golf Swing," Nelson perfected the technique of leading his downswing with a powerful leg drive. Nelson, who possessed a graceful and powerful swing, advised golfers to swing the club as if they were driving on the highway at 60, neither too slow nor too fast. However, he recommended occasionally speeding up to 70 mph, but never faster. If you want to unlearn the *hit impulse*, imitate Byron Nelson's swing.

Presently, the USGA uses a second-generation version of Iron Byron. The original Iron Byron is on display at The USGA Museum in Liberty Corner, New Jersey. According to the USGA's *Golf Journal*, Iron Byron's driver attains speeds of 130 mph and invariably snaps every 9,000 swings. Iron Byron's distance and accuracy are so precise that the USGA several times during the summer replaces the small area of turf where 2,000 range balls land each day.

Iron Byron consists of a five-foot pedestal equipped with one swiveling metal arm, hinged joints to replicate the elbow and wrist, and an adjustable sleeve to grip the club. Unlike bipedal golfers who ascribe two slightly different swing paths in their backswing and downswing, Iron Byron ascribes one swing path.

Iron Byron, a swing robot having only one arm and one leg, can teach you how to use your lead arm, lead wrist, and lead shoulder to generate angular velocity, but it can't teach you how to use your torso, hips, and legs to shift your weight and pivot.

Furthermore, it can't teach you to lower your center of gravity (i.e., drop vertically) in your transition. The human body, equipped with innumerable bones, muscles, and joints and an intricate central nervous system, is far more complex than a mechanical robot.

Iron Byron is more than a swing machine. It's a physical model that reduces the swing to mechanical movements based on scientific laws and principles. But the golf swing is not a robotic movement. The golf swing—akin to a dance step—is a dynamic movement that merges art and science, aesthetics and biomechanics.

Iron Byron serves as a useful model for auto assembly plants that require bionic hands and arms to weld joints, fasten bolts, and spray-paint fenders uniformly and precisely.

However, golfers are not assembly-line robots with bionic hands and arms.

Another swing model emerged in 1969 when Homer Kelley, a Boeing engineering consultant, published *The Golf Machine*. In 1941, Kelley became obsessed with golf. In his very first round, Kelley shot a dismal 116. Six months later, after applying engineering and scientific principles to his swing, he shot a 77 on a 7,000-yard course in Tacoma, Washington.

Subsequently, Kelley embarked on a 14-year quest to write a scientific swing manual for instructors and players by examining hundreds of expert golf swings, interviewing scores of instructors, and applying relevant scientific laws and principles.

Kelley aptly recognized golf's major problem: *Golf is poorly learned, taught, and played.* To solve this problem, Kelley self-published a 241-page scientific treatise using jargon and buzz words and applying physics, geometry, and biomechanics to analyze the swing. Golfers have both applauded and criticized Kelley's book.

Kelley revealed three shot-making fundamentals consonant with the laws of geometry and physics: (1) a stationary head, balance, and rhythm, (2) a flat lead wrist at impact, and (3) pressure-point lag along a straight swing plane. Kelley identified 24 swing components that can be executed in many different combinations. Before his death, Kelley established his The Golfing Machine (TGM) Program that tests, certifies, and issues degrees to qualified instructors.

In the 18th century, many people considered Sir Isaac Newton "The Christ of Science." In the 21st century, TGM instructors consider Homer Kelley "The Christ of Golf."

Kelley's belief—"Why trust instinct when there is science?"—summarizes his scientific and analytical model for teaching and learning the swing. *The Golf Machine*, despite its cult-like status, is a prime example of obfuscation by complexity and prolixity. As Emperor Josef II famously said about Mozart's *The Marriage of Figaro*: "Entirely, too many notes!"

In the late 1980s, kinesiologist Ralph Mann introduced another swing model. Mann used a computer to produce his "Model Pro Swing" by capturing and digitizing on high-speed film the swing images of 54 Tour pros. Mann produced a theoretical or computer swing model similar to Kelley's machine model. However, computer and machine models are only models.

There are many other respected swing models, including Moe Norman's *Natural Swing*, Theodore Jorgenson's *Physics Model*, Sasho MacKenzie and Eric Sprigings's *3-D Model*, and Steven Nesbit & Monika Serrano's *3-D Kinematic & Kinetic Model*.

Models play an important role in advancing scientific thinking. Scientists create models to explain and clarify complex mechanisms. The best scientific models are accepted when they've been properly tested and refined. However, models, especially swing models, are replicas of reality, not reality itself. Models are representations of truths.

Modeling highly complex, tightly coupled systems—consisting of intricate, hidden, and interdependent components interacting in baffling ways—is highly problematic.

Instructors have represented aspects of the golf swing in terms of rocking and throwing a softball underhand, hurling a discus, swinging a weight on a string, skipping a rock, chopping wood, hammering a nail, driving a wedge under a door frame, taking a slap shot, pounding a tent stake, catapulting a stone, swinging a baseball bat at the ground, pulling down on a bell rope, and snapping a whip. However, these are representations, analogies, comparisons, or approximations designed to make the strange *familiar*.

Why do metaphors foster efficient learning? The use of metaphors in the learning process is rooted in the *Theory of Neural Re-Use*. This theory posits that metaphors and the concepts they represent employ the same neural circuits in the brain. Metaphors, which compare the *known* with the *unknown* (i.e., hammering a nail and hitting a golf ball), simplify and clarify complex concepts.

Neuroscientist Michael Anderson, in his article *"Neural Re-Use: A Functional Organizational Principle of the Brain,"* claims that the brain reuses neural circuitry for various cognitive functions. He writes, ". . . it is quite common for neural circuits established for one purpose to be *exapted* (exploited, recycled, redeployed) during evolution or normal development, and be put to different uses, often without losing their original functions."

After you establish neural circuits to initiate and learn an original action (e.g., hammering a nail), you *reuse* them to initiate and acquire new and different actions (e.g., hitting a golf ball). Metaphors, which recycle your neural circuitry, help you acquire new skills.

The golf swing is a complex system that incorporates other complex systems (e.g., mechanical, neurological, psychological, anatomical, kinesthetic). Mathematician Stephen Wolfram (*A New Kind of Science*) uses the term "computational irreducibility" to denote complex systems that defy computer simulation. Essentially, Wolfram asserts that certain things and events defy precise modeling and exact simulation.

For example, computer simulations fail to make accurate predictions about climate change—a complex system embedded in ecological, human, social, biological, chemical, and many other systems. I'm not saying that all forms of "computational irreducibility" are the same. I'm saying that designing an exact model for a complex system containing many other complex systems is a daunting task.

Physicist Neil Gershenfeld said, "The most common misunderstanding about science is that scientists seek and find truth. They don't—they make and test models. . . . Making sense of anything means making models that can predict outcomes and accommodate observations. Truth is a model." Picasso stated, "Art is a lie that helps us see the truth."

Unfortunately, Lawrence Livermore Labs, Bell Labs, and Berkeley Labs do not test swing models, theories, and methodologies. Therefore, you must test and develop swing models on your own. Select a swing model based on sound principles, factual proof, solid evidence, and proven results—not on testimonials and blind faith.

Moreover, stop trying to discover the hidden swing secrets of Hogan, Nelson, or Iron Byron. Stop trying to become someone else. Find the hidden secrets within your own swing. Become you. Your unique neural firing patterns and brain cells belong exclusively to you. What resides inside PGA Tour pros resides in them—not you.

Develop a swing consonant with your skill level, physical parameters, learning style, cognitive ability, and goals to achieve the common denominators in all exemplary swings: *balance, tempo,* and *rhythm.*

It's doubtful whether one specific model has a lock on reality. To improve your learning and enhance your skill sets, integrate several models, especially opposing models. You won't learn much from people who view things exactly as you do. Within golf there are many competing swing models and methodologies. Since there is no perfect model, find ones that suit you.

Transcend the limits of binary choices or dualistic (i.e., either-or) thinking. Simply stated, integrate opposing or complementary swing models. Reap the benefits of several alternative swing models. If you foolishly settle on one swing model, you'll ignore the multiple benefits of competing models.

Selecting between alternative approaches creates tension. Integrating alternative approaches, like a river flowing between opposite banks, creates equilibrium, composure, and flow. Herman Hesse, in *Siddhartha*, wrote, "The river has taught me to listen; you will learn from it too. The river knows everything; one can learn everything from it." You'll achieve flow when you think like a river.

The American novelist F. Scott Fitzgerald wrote, "The test of first-class intelligence is the ability to hold two opposing ideas in mind at the same time and still retain the ability to function. One should, for example, be able to see that things are hopeless, yet be determined to make them otherwise."

In *The Opposable Mind* (2007), Roger Martin writes, "Opposing models, in fact, are the richest source of new insight into a problem. We learn nothing from someone who sees the problem exactly as we do." Each swing model reflects a different perspective on reality. On the battlefield of competing swing models, experts insist that their theories and practices represent ultimate truth. Consequently, advocates ignore, dismiss, and reject the attributes of rival models. Today, little or no commerce exists among rival swing theories.

Perhaps a perfect swing model—universally endorsed by PGA instructors, neuroscientists, psychologists, physicists, engineers, and other brilliant thinkers—will eventually emerge. Until then, swing mechanics will reside in separate silos owned by self-interested proponents. Therefore, integrate the best aspects among all available models.

The absence of an ideal model is an occupational hazard to golfers. Therefore, be wary of flawed models. Suppose that Elvis Presley is your cultural icon. However, shitty genes have cursed you with patterned baldness. Hence, you can't ask your barber to give you a "Rockabilly" hairstyle so you can swoop your hair in front of your eyes on the dance floor to drive the women wild. Some models are not for you.

To play like Ben Hogan, you don't need Hogan's swing. You need Hogan's talent, personality, mind, and brain. To write like Ernest Hemingway, you don't need his typing skills. You need Hemingway's talent, personality, mind, and brain. Personalize, individualize, and customize to become your own guru.

Paul Runyan

Ernest Jones, Tommy Armour, Bob Toski, John Jacobs, and Dave Stockton have been not only great golfers but also great teachers. Another great player who was also a great teacher was Paul Runyan. He won twenty-nine PGA Tour events and mentored Gene Littler, Phil Rodgers, Mickey Wright, and Tommy Aaron.

Paul Runyan—standing 5'7" and weighing 125 pounds—was called "Little Poison" for his diminutive size and deadly short game. Runyan won the PGA Championship in 1934 and 1938. Despite Sam Snead's 75-yard driving advantage, Runyan won the 1938 PGA Championship. Up 8 holes with 7 to play, Runyan recorded the most lopsided match-play victory in the event's 43-year history. (The PGA Championship was conducted in match play between 1916 and 1957.)

In a used bookstore many years ago, I found a worn copy of *How to Solve Your Golf Problems* (1964). The book contained practical lessons by Byron Nelson, Jackie Burke, Paul Runyan, Horton Smith, and Johnny Revolta. Paul Runyan's lessons did the trick for me.

In Runyan's discussion of "sclaffing"—a Scottish links term for hitting fat shots—he writes, "Hitting the ground first is bad on two counts. First, it slows down the clubhead an instant before its all-important contact with the ball. Second, it produces poor contact as grass or earth come between the clubface and the ball."

Runyan stressed the correct setup angles for the club shaft, forearms, and spine. To hit consistent and accurate shots, according to Runyan, you must establish and maintain the same *forearm-to-shaft angle for all clubs*. He writes, "Maintain the same arm-club angle at impact that you assumed at address." This was a major wake-up call.

Physicist John Wheeler, who coined the term *black hole*, said, "If you haven't found something strange during the day, it hasn't been much of a day." When I realized that I was hitting fat shots because of my variable forearm-to-shaft angles, I discovered a black hole in my swing.

Why is it so important to maintain the forearm-to-shaft angle? Since the club rotates around the spine, any change in the position of the arms and club relative to the spine is problematic. It goes back to systems theory. Undue variability in tightly coupled complex systems—especially in your intricate setup components—induces breakdowns.

Guided by Runyan's precepts, I detected three major flaws in my setup: (1) my hands at address—causing the shaft to point above my beltline—were too high, (2) my hands were too far away from my thighs, and (3) my left forearm—instead of forming a 145-degree angle at the base of my left thumb with the shaft—formed a straight line. In brief, my setup was screwy.

From setup to impact and from driver to wedge, Tour players retain the *same* forearm-to-shaft angle relative to their spine. This was a revelation. Setting the *same* forearm-to-shaft angle for all clubs simplifies the swing. Conversely, setting a *different* forearm-to-shaft angle for each club complicates the swing. Tour pros, who adopt the same forearm-to-shaft angle for all clubs, employ *one* swing. Hackers employ *multiple* swings.

I wrongly assumed that each club—adjusted for ball position, stance width, hip bend, and spine angle—also demanded a different forearm-to-shaft angle. Big mistake! *Runyan taught me to assume and retain essentially the same forearm-to-shaft angle for all clubs.*

Runyan didn't say that Tour pros set up with exactly the same amount of hip bend and spine angle for all clubs. Obviously, driver and wedge require a slightly different hip/waist bend and spine angle. Rather, Runyan said that Tour pros set the same *forearm-to-shaft angle* for all clubs. Amateurs alter their forearm-to-shaft angle during their swing by arching their wrists and changing their grip pressure. Tour pros don't.

One more thing! Runyan didn't say that the address and impact positions are identical. Clearly, the address-fix and impact-fix are very different. Rather, Runyan said that the forearm-to-shaft angle is essentially the same from address to impact.

Researchers have recently confirmed Runyan's assertions. Computer analysis indicates that Ben Hogan's forearm-to-shaft angle was 149 degrees at setup and 154 degrees at impact; Sam Snead's was 146 degrees at setup and 144 degrees at impact. Studies now reveal that the forearm-to-shaft angle among approximately two hundred male and female Tour pros ranges between 140 and 149 degrees. The average forearm-to-shaft angle for Tour pros is 144 degrees.

The difference between the forearm-to-shaft angle at address and impact among Tour pros is only plus or minus 2 degrees. The correlation between maintaining a consistent forearm-to-shaft angle for all clubs *and* hitting consistent and accurate shots may be golf's best-kept secret.

Homer Kelley, author of *The Golfing Machine* (1969), compressed his thinking into one lucid sentence: "The secret of golf is sustaining the 'Line of Compression.'" To sustain the Line of Compression, you must set and retain the same forearm-to-shaft angle for all clubs, as Runyan insists.

Jimmy Ballard famously said, "The golf swing is all about angles." Accordingly, setting the forearm-to-shaft at approximately 144 degrees may be the game's most important yet most-ignored angle.

To correctly establish your setup, lower your hands, flex your knees slightly, bend at the waist, and position the club toe-up. (Slide a credit card halfway down the clubface to ensure the club rests toe-up on the ground.) As a rule of thumb, set up by positioning your chin between your feet and eight inches behind the ball.

Paul Runyan advised his pupils to *under-reach* (i.e., hover the clubhead above the ball) rather than *over-reach* (i.e., rest the clubhead on the ground). Overreaching (1) shortens your swing radius by lowering the suspension point at the base of your neck and (2) inhibits a free-flowing swing by distorting the club's true weight. Overreaching promotes an unnatural motion and produces inconsistent shots. Underreaching promotes a natural motion and produces consistent shots.

Most important, assuming a forearm-to-shaft setup angle of approximately 144 degrees precocks your wrists. In a swing lasting only 1.4 seconds, most expert golfers precock their wrists at setup. With your wrists precocked, you simply need to lift your arms, fold your elbows, and retain your forearm-to-shaft angle relative to your spine.

Tour pros may not know their exact forearm-to-shaft angle. After years of coaching and deliberate practice, however, Tour pros have developed the requisite neural circuitry to set up the same way each time. With deliberate practice and self-monitoring, you'll be able to do the same. However, setting up the same way every time demands cognitive bandwidth.

Most amateurs use variable and incorrect positions for their hands, arms, and club relative to their spine at setup. Haphazard and random setups breed inconsistency. Tour pros reduce their setup variables. Amateurs increase their setup variables.

Paul Runyan won his first PGA Championship in 1934 at The Park Country Club, presently known as Delaware Park, founded in 1903 in Buffalo, New York. Whenever I drive past Delaware Park, located near my home, I pay homage to Paul Runyan.

When I win the Megabucks, I plan to erect a life-size statue of Paul Runyan at the entrance to Delaware Park. In fact, I'll pay extra for the sculptor to include Runyan's trademark eyeglasses. If Paterson, New Jersey, can erect a life-size statue of Lou Costello holding a baseball bat, Buffalo, New York, can erect a life-size statue of Paul Runyan holding a golf club.

Confirmation Bias

To help you take some trash to the dump, you called your shifty, undershowered brother-in-law, Richie. Referring to Richie as a horse's reproductive organ would be a compliment.

Last week Richie borrowed $78 to buy new sneakers. (Goodwill and Amvets don't carry size 16.5.) Richie, who owes you money, will never call you back.

Confirmation bias—based on intuitions, prejudices, and assumptions—denotes flawed thinking. When confirmation bias shapes your thinking, you're a prisoner of your own beliefs. Consequently, you'll ignore contradictory evidence and critical investigation. Since search engines are the epitome of confirmation bias, why use them to validate or prove your beliefs?

Maintaining illusions is easy and reassuring. Investigating critically is difficult and demanding. Psychologist Leon Festinger, "The Father of Cognitive Dissonance," wrote, ". . . people interpret information to fit what they already believe."

Daniel Kahneman, a Yale psychologist, claims that even highly intelligent, well-educated people exhibit confirmation bias. Many people, even when they're confronted with contradictory and incontrovertible evidence, will refuse to change their opinions. Kahneman calls this mode of thinking "ideologically motivated cognition."

During a recent radio interview, a prominent university astrophysicist stated, "Even if you could scientifically prove to me that UFOs exist, I still wouldn't believe it." That's classic confirmation bias.

If you believe what you've always believed, you'll never improve. Award-winning theoretical physicist Richard Feynman embraced uncertainty. He wrote, "We are trying to prove ourselves wrong as quickly as possible because only in that way can we find progress." To achieve breakthroughs, prove to yourself your swing is flawed.

Golfers, who lack the time and expertise to examine a range of diverse and contradictory evidence, let others do their thinking. Be especially wary of experts who impart simplistic binary advice, such as using a strong vs. weak grip, an open vs. closed stance or a one-plane vs. two-plane swing. The golf swing—containing many gray areas—defies simplistic dichotomies.

Professor Wing Suen, in "The Self-Perpetuation of Biased Beliefs," observed that people tend to seek advice from like-minded individuals. He states, "This means that a person who begins with some initial bias has a large chance to become even more biased after learning the evidence that has been filtered by third parties. In other words, *bias tends to beget bias* and pre-existing divergence of opinion will become more polarized given the selective choice of evidence." Weigh contradictory evidence and identify biases.

To recognize and purge your illusions and biases, continually refresh your beliefs. Flawed swings flow from flawed, lazy, and delusional thinking. If you're a cognitive miser—if you don't explore and test new approaches—you'll never grow.

Internet and social media channels that provide golfers with quick and uncritical information epitomize confirmation bias. Unless you self-scrutinize your thinking, you'll perpetuate your ignorance and incompetence. The only thing worse than ignorance and incompetence is passionate ignorance and incompetence.

In the 1999 film *The Matrix*, the main character, Neo, is asked to choose between a blue pill and a red pill. The blue pill keeps him in an illusory and happy life *inside* the Matrix. The red pill thrusts him into a challenging and realistic life *outside* the Matrix.

Golfers face a similar choice. Golfers who remain in their illusionary golf matrix and languish for decades keep taking blue pills. Blue pills will perpetuate your repeated failures.

To exit your illusionary golf matrix—where you can challenge, explore, and test new methodologies and approaches—start taking red pills. Red pills will sustain your efforts to improve. To escape the matrix of fake theories, errant practices, and misguided experts, keep an ample supply of red pills in your golf bag.

Abraham Lincoln intentionally staffed his cabinet with politicians who held opposing views. When Lincoln had to make a key decision, he encouraged vigorous debate and discussion. The same applies to you. When you make decisions regarding your backswing, swing plane, and pivot, for example, explore and test alternative views.

Your brain, which runs on only 40 watts of power, has little energy to spare. Consequently, your low-energy brain defaults to familiar and consensual notions. Unfortunately, breakthroughs and epiphanies rarely flow from familiar and consensual notions.

To see things differently, banish your predictable perceptions. Jolt your mind with novel approaches, theories, and practices. Then test your findings. Novelty often unshackles past perceptions, triggers fresh judgments, and induces new learning. Novel approaches will arouse your awareness, reconfigure your thinking, and rewire your brain.

Uncertainty generates an alert or threat response in your limbic system. Your brain avoids uncertainty and craves certainty. Given the game's fickle and unpredictable nature, golfers cling to biases, myths, and preconceptions. Confronted with uncertainty, your brain—a neuronal predictive machine equipped with a unique reward or pleasure center—steers toward confirmation biases.

You can mitigate—but never eliminate—confirmation bias. Cosmologist Stephen Hawking said, "The greatest enemy of knowledge is not ignorance; it's the illusion of knowledge." Change your mind . . . to change your brain . . . to change your swing.

When Richie returned your call, you were thunderstruck. He has your $78 and wants to help you. It turns out that your confirmation bias about Richie was dead wrong.

The Mind's Eye

The most gifted scientists, artists, and athletes have great imaginations. Einstein, who considered imagination more important than knowledge, said, "I'm enough of an artist to draw freely on my imagination, which I think is more important than knowledge. Knowledge is limited. Imagination encircles the world." To realize your golf potential, engage your imagination.

Imagination—your mind's eye—requires no sensory input to produce creative images, startling metaphors, ingenious cognitive maps, and inventive schemas. Your mind's eye is fundamental to learning.

Cicero referenced the "mind's eye" when he advised ancient orators to use only simple and familiar similes in their discourse. He wrote, "The eyes of the mind are more easily directed to those objects which we have seen than to those objects which we have only heard."

People conjure mental images with varying degrees of vividness. Approximately 2 percent of all people who are unable to visualize things in their mind have a condition called "congenital aphantasia." Without your mind's eye, you're *mentally blind*. In 1880, psychologist Francis Galton wrote a famous paper titled "Statistics of Mental Imagery," in which he expounded on people's varying ability to form mental pictures.

Recent studies indicate that mental imagery helps eight-year-old kids to remember what they read. Pupils who employ mental imagery develop their vocabulary two and half times faster than those who use only auditory cues. If you can't imagine, you can't learn.

Your powers of imagination and memory are controlled mainly in the brain's neocortex and thalamus. The neural link between imagination and memory allows you to recollect things vividly. Neuroscientists using MRI technology assert that imagining and remembering send blood to identical parts of the brain. Simply put, imagination and memory are interrelated.

Since imagination is fundamental to learning, golfers must be able to create and recall a mental swing-map. Steven Pinker, a cognitive scientist, claims that we represent our world through mental images, not through words and thoughts. Mental images are cognitive shortcuts that process, interpret, understand, simplify, and organize complex information.

To improve your swing, employ subconscious sensations and mental images—not conscious thoughts and verbal self-talk.

To learn the golf swing, activate your imagination. Construct a picture in your mind's eye. Imagine yourself as a 3-D spatial structure. With your eyes closed, experience the proprioceptive movements of your body and club. In your mind's eye, imprint a lasting image of the perfect golf swing. Your ability to conjure mental images is the operational principle of human intelligence. When you conjure the correct images, words will follow. Words lose their meaning when they get disconnected from images.

In 1948, Edward Tolman, a cognitive psychologist, introduced the concept of "cognitive mapping"—imaginative spatial images. A cognitive map, which internalizes an external reality in your imagination, allows you to acquire, understand, simplify, clarify, store, and recall complex information.

Neuroscientists speculate that mental mapping or spatial cognition is largely a function of the brain's hippocampus. The hippocampus is the region most affected by those afflicted with Alzheimer's, dementia, and memory loss. The hippocampus, which organizes experience and integrates spatial and non-spatial information from different areas of the brain, is where mental mapping occurs.

If you don't know the best driving route between Toronto and DC, you must employ your car's navigation system. Since not all routes are equal, you must select the safest, fastest, and quickest route. The same criteria apply to selecting your optimal swing map.

If you don't know how to hit a golf ball from tee to green, you need a viable swing map in your mind's eye. However, not all swing maps are equal. Some swing maps are incomplete, inaccurate, unclear, and confusing. Therefore, you must employ your intellect, experience, and imagination to select the right one.

Many instructors offer incomplete swing maps that emphasize only one segment of swing, such as the "impact zone." Since impact happens uncontrollably in 1/1200th of a second, a swing map that emphasizes the impact zone for novice golfers is problematic.

I'm not telling you to ignore the impact zone in your swing map. I'm telling you to focus on what happens *before, during,* and *after* impact. I'm telling you that the golf swing is a complex, tightly coupled system consisting of interdependent components. I'm telling you to adopt a holistic swing map.

A cognitive swing map that emphasizes one particular segment, such as the impact zone, is tantamount to keeping a neighborhood street map of Manhattan on your GPS screen during your nine-hour drive from Toronto to New York City.

When I formulated a cognitive map based on Mike Austin's "Figure 7" concept—in which the lead arm forms the lower member of the 7 and the shoulder girdle forms the upper member—I had an epiphany. This swing map enabled me to understand, visualize, execute, and repeat a low-maintenance swing. Visualizing the figure 7, I solved golf's most vexing problem, namely, how to blend the turning of my body and the swinging of my arms.

When Archimedes discovered a simple method to determine the density of an object, he exclaimed, "Eureka!"— literally meaning "I found it!" When I discovered a simple method to blend my body-pivot and arm-swing, I exclaimed, "Wow-We-Wow."

Two famous American architects—along with other imaginative thinkers—have shaped my thinking and learning. Buckminster Fuller, who invented the geodesic dome, inspired me to develop a simple and effective swing. Fuller wrote, "Do more with less." Frank Lloyd Wright, a self-taught master with a pioneering spirit, inspired me to think innovatively. Wright wrote, "An architect's most useful tools are an eraser at the drafting board and a wrecking bar at the site."

A Yardstick for Failure

If you can hit only six or seven good shots for every ten, you're hindered by flawed thinking and bad habits. If so, consider inventorying your shots over several rounds. Determine what percentage of your shots is acceptable. Your percentage of bad shots constitutes your yardstick for failure. The higher the percentage of bad shots, the more work you need to do.

Don't expect some golf guru to put your game together. Put yourself together. Stop sugarcoating your golf mess. If you think your game is as smooth as a ball bearing, you'll never grow.

Dramatic growth doesn't begin when you're reading a book, viewing a video, meditating on a yoga mat, or walking alone on the beach. It happens after a bad round in the throes of anger, frustration, disappointment, and failure. It happens when you resolve to change what you're doing. Appointments for growth arise from chaos and despair.

All behavioral and cognitive changes entail risk. A major issue facing golfers is risk-assessment. You need a measured, balanced, logical, and scientific approach to change what you're thinking and doing. Growth depends on your ability to select the best swing methodologies among many options.

Your mindset determines your thinking. Your thinking determines your swing. Your swing determines your game. And your game determines peace of mind.

Before you can assess your swing, assess your cognitive framework. If you're satisfied with your game—distance off the tee, greens in regulation, putts per round, and ball-striking ability—don't change a thing. However, if you're dissatisfied with your game, change your thinking and doing.

To initiate change, assess your risk-propensity. In sum, weigh the potential gains and losses associated with making swing changes. Are you patient and persistent enough to see your game get worse before it improves? Do you want a *swing-change* in the form of a major breakthrough or a *swing-adjustment* in the form of a quick fix? Establish a context for your swing changes.

Dr. Amos Tversky, a Stanford University researcher, studied the risk propensities of decision-makers. Tversky found that most people avoid making changes to avert negative results. In sum, people tend to change their habits to avoid losses rather than to achieve gains.

"The threat of a loss," Tversky writes, "has a greater impact on a decision than the possibility of an equivalent gain." No wonder stymied golfers cling to flawed methodologies.

Don't be risk-averse or risk-prone. Be risk-balanced. Assess the risks associated with making swing changes. To foster growth, you must take calculated risks.

Why You Have a Brain

The only reason you have a brain—according to your mother-in-law—is to fix her garbage grinder, hot water heater, garage door opener, lawn mower, shower fixture, electric hair dryer, smoke alarm, washing machine, lawn trimmer, closet door, towel rack, kitchen dimmer switch, Rascal Scooter, television remote, vacuum cleaner, and Fedders air conditioner purchased at Goodwill in 1997 for $23.

Neuroscientists researching human and animal behavior assert that the brain serves one primary function: *To produce adaptable and complex movements.* This is an important finding for golfers.

Dr. Daniel Wolpert, a University of Cambridge neurobiologist, studies how the brain controls movement. In a published interview conducted at The Cold Spring Harbor Symposia on Quantitative Biology in 2014, Wolpert stated: "I work on how the brain controls movement. Movements are fundamental to our existence. The only way we can affect the world around us is through the contractions of muscles; there's no other way to improve our survival. It's important to remember that things like sensory, memory, and cognitive processes are important to drive or suppress future movements. The beauty of working on movement is that you have to work on the whole system. It's the final output."

Wolpert mentions the humble sea squirt to illustrate his key point. Early in its life, the rudimentary sea squirt swims around the ocean before it permanently attaches itself to a rock. Since it will never leave that rock, the sea squirt digests its own brain and nervous system for nourishment. In sum, immobile organisms don't need brains. Golfers who don't use their brains are analogous to immobilized sea squirts.

Dr. Wolpert claims the brain's ability to record childhood memories or apprehend the sensory stimuli of a flower have no evolutionary advantage, since such neural input is unrelated to movement.

Humans can build robots capable of defeating humans in chess matches. But humans can't build robots capable of manipulating chess pieces with the digital dexterity of a five-year-old. Artificial brains can perform singular and directed tasks like spot welding on an auto assembly line. However, only human brains can execute multiple, flexible, nuanced, and refined movements.

Learning complex skills involves the activation of different motor-memories. Take note of what Wolpert is saying here: "What we've just found out is that the motor memory you activate now depends not only on what you've done in the past, but what you're going to do in the future. If you have a consistent follow-through after an action, you store that in one motor memory. If you have different follow-throughs, however, you store them in different motor memories, and therefore don't consolidate them. What we've shown is that part of the reason you want to follow-through is to store everything into one motor memory."

The golf swing—a dynamic, complex, and controlled movement involving 600 muscles—possesses infinite variability. There are thousands of possible muscular contractions in every swing. Your inconsistent golf swings, compared to the consistent swings of Tour pros, contain a high level of variability. In brief, Tour pros have less variability in their swings.

According to neuroscientists, your brain controls movements by remembering past events and predicting subsequent events. Your brain creates each swing anew by accessing a vast assortment of past motor-memories and by processing a rich data field of immediate sensory stimuli. To develop an effective and repeatable swing, you must reduce your swing variables. To minimize the amount of cognitive interference (i.e., "noise"), you must simplify your swing.

If you could observe the intricate firing patterns among the 86 billion neurons controlling the contractions of 600 muscles in a swing lasting 1.4 seconds, you would appreciate golf's variability problem. You can minimize—but not eliminate—variability. Every swing is planned and executed differently.

To minimize variability in pursuit of a low-maintenance and consistent swing, focus on the split second between impact and follow-through. Use your brain's blood supply to minimize the variability during this critical swing interval.

Neuroscientists assert that your brain's primary function is to plan and execute complex movements. Use your brain—every golfer's best training aid—to develop a consistent and effective swing. Develop a swing based on an effective and simple paradigm, on reduced variability, and on a proper follow-through.

Breathing

Among all athletic activities, golf may be the most ironic. On one hand, golfers—exposed to moderate exercise, fresh air, natural beauty, and pleasant social interactions—experience relaxation and bliss. On the other hand, golfers—subjected to repeated failure, limited improvement, erratic shot patterns, and embarrassing public displays—experience stress and frustration.

Golf, depending on your outlook and coping skills, can "bliss you out" or "stress you out." Golf is neither positive nor negative, blissful nor stressful. Golf is whatever you make it—whatever you create for it.

The simple truth is that millions of golfers experience high levels of stress, anger, and depression. Excessive stress to a failed golfer is what excessive glucose is to a diabetic. Both levels are deadly.

Stress constricts your blood flow, clouds your thinking, destroys your composure, quickens your swing, and sabotages your performance. Conversely, relaxation enhances your blood flow, sharpens your thinking, sustains your composure, slows down your swing, and enhances your performance.

If you can't control your stress, stress will control you. Here's the good news. You can control stress by simply changing your breathing patterns. Yogic breathing techniques will improve your mental and physical well-being. However, don't take my word for this. Test this technique for yourself.

First, position the tip of your tongue against the roof of your mouth. This will quiet the ceaseless and distracting "monkey chatter" in your brain's frontal cortex. Second, breathe through your abdomen, not your chest. That's it!

To play well, empty and quiet your mind. Quieting your mind, an alien notion to most golfers, is best expressed in the following Zen paradox: "When you're empty, you're full." This may be one of golf's biggest secrets. When thoughts swirl around your mind like snowflakes, you become stressed, unfocused, and rushed. To calm your mind, simply breathe through your abdomen.

Abdominal breathing quiets the nerve switchboard residing in your solar plexus. Your solar plexus, containing a network of nerves in your "abdominal brain," is located behind your stomach. The network of nerves in your solar plexus transmits energy-messages of stress, anger, and depression throughout your body.

Rhythmic abdominal breathing which inhibits negative energy (1) oxygenates your brain, (2) shortens your stress cycle, and (3) normalizes your heart rate and blood pressure, thereby allowing you to play better. Oxygenating your blood *adds* pain-relieving endorphins and *inhibits* stress-inducing hormones.

Slow, deep, and rhythmic abdominal breathing calms your sympathetic nervous system and regulates the functioning of your inner organs. Inhale and exhale slowly and rhythmically through your nostrils as if you're drinking air. Then deflate your lungs as if you were blowing out a birthday candle.

To focus on your breathing, thereby excluding all distractions, employ a mantra, for example, "I'm inhaling calmness and exhaling tension."

Stunted golfers with fast swings and rapid breathing tend to *hold* their breath during their downswing. Adroit golfers with slow swings and shallow breathing tend to *expel* breath during their downswing. Timing your in-breaths and out-breaths will smooth out your swing.

Tom Watson uses a unique breathing method he adapted from skeet shooting. He advises golfers to do the following: (1) inhale deeply, (2) exhale deeply, (3) inhale deeply again, (4) exhale half of your breath—and hold it, (5) exhale the rest during the swing.

In *Zen in the Art of Archery*, Eugen Herrigel stressed the importance of proper breathing to enhance performance, expand consciousness, and reduce stress. To unclutter your mind and relax your muscles, periodically shift your focus from *swing techniques* to *breathing techniques*.

Intellect vs. Intelligence

Yesterday, you took a 45-minute golf lesson at The Purgatory Golf Center from a PGA professional. You wanted the pro to fix your slice. So he filmed your swing and compared it frame-by-frame with Dustin Johnson's.

You overrotate your hips, come over the top, stand up in your downswing, lose your balance, counterrotate both forearms, steeply tilt your shoulders, and cup your left wrist at impact. Plus, you have a shitty grip. Then he biomechanically demonstrated his own swing in slow motion and exhibited the delivery positions of the top Tour pros. When he stopped to take a breath, your time was up. He'll fix your slice during your next lesson.

This golf lesson was *intellect-based*—not *intelligence-based*. To learn golf, you must integrate intellect and intelligence. The terms are not synonymous.

Intellect denotes the rational process of knowing, analyzing, memorizing, and categorizing factual information. *Intelligence* denotes the mental faculty that engages the feelings behind your actions and decisions.

In his article "Intellect and Intelligence" published in *Psychology Today*, Graham Collier writes, "Intellect (Fact) and Intelligence (Feeling) determine the existential course of one's journey through life. In other words, the strength of your feel-ings—derived from your intelligence—dictates how you eval-uate and respond to factual information—derived from your intellect."

Jiddu Krishnamurti writes, "Training the intellect does not result in intelligence. Rather, intelligence comes into being when one acts in perfect harmony, both intellectually and emotionally. . . . Intellect is merely thought functioning inde-pendently of emotion. When intellect, irrespective of emotion, is trained in any particular direction, one may have great intel-lect, but one does not have intelligence . . ."

To hone your golf intelligence, think counterintuitively. Shivas Irons, the fictional golfer in Michael Murphy's *Golf in the Kingdom* (1971), states, "Our relationship to paradox is a barometer of our enlightenment."

The golf swing is paradoxical, counterintuitive, and unnat-ural. In golf, you swing slowly and easily to generate power. You swing down to hit the ball up. You relax your wrists to accelerate and release the club. You turn your back to the tar-get to propel the ball at the target. You swing on a curved path to hit the ball on a straight path.

Ignorant and nonathletic people often make superb golf-ers. Conversely, intelligent and athletic people often make atrocious golfers. Go figure!

Your intellect—your mind's analytical and active side—helps you think verbally and deeply to understand swing mechanics. Factual information and self-talk trigger the intel-lect. However, kinesthetic feelings and images trigger your intelligence. Intelligence, your mind's instinctive and passive side, fosters feelings to help you perform spontaneously and subconsciously.

Don't overthink everything. When you've had a string of pars, for example, quiet your intellect and engage your intelligence. Enter the *zone,* experience *flow,* and become blissfully ignorant.

Merge intellect and intelligence when you're on the green. Activate your *intellect* by processing factual information. Align the Titleist logo with your putting line. Assess the distance of your putt. Inspect your putt from four sides. Observe the green's uphill contour, left break, and its various spike marks. Inspect the damage around the cup.

Next, activate your *intelligence* by processing your feelings, apprehensions, and expectations. Assess the feelings associated with stroking the putt squarely, stroking it too hard, visualizing the break, recalling other clutch putts, and imagining the ball dying in the hole. Simply stated, merge facts and feelings—intellect and intelligence.

When you merge thinking and feeling—intellect and intelligence—you access harmony, balance, and rhythm. Intellect or intelligence alone limits you. Intellect and intelligence together expand you.

Great Expectations

During The Masters, when spring flowers bloom, your golfing expectations soar. You aspire to lower your handicap, improve your ball-striking, develop a rhythmic putting stroke, and relocate your mother-in-law to Nome, Alaska.

In "The Waste Land," T.S. Eliot wrote, "April is the cruelest month." Spring creates the illusion of growth and renewal. However, few golfers actually experience growth and renewal. "If growth is the only evidence of life," as Cardinal John Henry Newman asserted, then most golfers are zombies.

According to The National Golf Foundation, the handicap of the average golfer has remained essentially the same for decades. Many top PGA instructors privately confess that relatively few golfers lower their handicaps or enhance their skill sets.

Unlike athletes engaged in karate, weight lifting, cycling, and other sports, golfers rarely experience steady improvement. Most golfers enjoy a short burst of growth during their first three years, then stagnate. The lack of growth among most golfers, despite their enormous expenditure of time, effort, and money, is the surest indication something's screwy in the way golf is being taught and learned.

USGA—whose motto is "For the good of the game"—should focus on the serious issue of failed teaching and learning—not on trivial issues like metal spikes on golf shoes and square grooves on wedges.

Cognitive psychologists have analyzed the failed performances of incompetent people. Researchers contend that incompetent people are unwilling and unable to monitor their ineptitude. Simply stated, incompetent people are performance-blind.

Two notable experiments help explain why America's 25 million golfers rarely improve. First, Justin Kruger and David Dunning—who published their findings in *The Journal of Personality and Social Psychology* in 1999—studied the domains of joke telling, logical reasoning, and English grammar. They found that performers who overestimated their performance in these domains achieved the lowest test scores.

Kruger and Dunning noted that the worst performers were least aware of (1) which test questions they answered incorrectly and (2) how poorly they performed overall. Here's the double whammy in all this. You need the same knowledge not only to *recognize* but also to *remedy* your failures.

Kruger and Dunning's findings have important implications for golfers. Incompetent performers tend to *overestimate* their proficiencies. Conversely, competent golfers tend to *underestimate* their proficiencies. "He who knows best," Thomas Jefferson stated, "knows how little he knows."

Second, Leo Rosenblit and Frank Keil in 2002 conducted a related study applicable to stymied golfers. Their study published in *The Journal of Cognitive Science* probes what they call the "Illusion of Explanatory Depth." In sum, incompetent people, convinced they understood how something works, when pressed for a clear and logical explanation can rarely furnish one.

Rosenblit and Keil asked their graduate students to explain the workings of flush toilets, bicycle derailleurs, and grandfather clocks. When subjects were asked to provide clear and logical explanations for how these devices worked, they couldn't deliver.

Golf pupils and instructors, exposed to a wealth of information, wrongly suppose they understand swing mechanics. Failure based on false information is the scourge of most golfers. Failed golfers don't know that they don't know. *Most golfers have just enough information to think they're right, but not enough information to know they're wrong.*

Researchers, like Dr. Wolfram Schultz, have studied the effects of performance expectations on the brain. Schultz, a Cambridge University neurologist, studied dopamine levels in the brain relative to one's expected rewards. In his article "Getting Formal with Dopamine and Reward" (in *Neuron*), Schultz asserts that dopamine levels increase when you anticipate and meet your expectations and decrease when you don't. If this is true, golfers must have the lowest dopamine levels on the planet.

In "Your Brain at Work" (*Psychology Today*), Dr. David Rock posits that you need high dopamine levels to focus properly. He writes, "You need good levels of dopamine to *hold* an idea in your prefrontal cortex. Positive expectations increase the levels of dopamine in the brain, and these increased levels make you more able to focus." To avoid disappointment, Rock thereby advises people to set modest and realistic expectations.

"Unmet expectations," Rock states, "are one of the most important experiences to avoid, as these generate the stronger threat response. . . . When you step back and look at all the possible outcomes this way, it makes sense to minimize one's expectations of positive rewards in most situations. Keeping an even keel about potential wins pays off."

At season's end when you've failed to lower your handicap, improve your ball-striking, and relocate your mother-in-law to Nome, Alaska, get a dopamine booster shot from your physician to escape the doldrums.

Neurogenesis

Golfers striving to generate new brain cells to enhance their skill sets owe an unpayable debt to the zebra fish. For the past twenty years, scientists have used zebra fish to study adult *neurogenesis*—the brain's ability to create new brain cells and generate new synaptic connections.

The zebra fish's unique capacity to (1) generate 6,000 new brain cells every 30 minutes, (2) reproduce rapidly, and (3) adapt to high-resolution microscopic analysis makes it an attractive subject for studying human brain cell development.

In their article "Neurogenesis in Zebra Fish: From Embryo to Adult," Rebecca Schmidt and her colleagues write, ". . . recent studies have shown that the mature zebra fish brain may also serve as a valuable model for the study of adult neurogenesis. Indeed, as early as the 1960s, first experiments suggested that new neurons are born in the hippocampus and the olfactory bulb of the adult mammalian brain. . . . It took, however, more than 20 years before neurogenesis in the adult mammalian brain became widely accepted."

People long believed that the adult human brain is incapable of generating brain cells. However, recent insights gained from studying zebra fish confirm that neurogenesis can replace brain cells destroyed by aging, drug abuse, and alcoholism. Moreover, Swedish neuroscientist Peter Eriksson and his team of researchers concluded that neurogenesis continues throughout your entire life.

Apparently, the adult brain can regenerate and replace dead and damaged brains cells. The functionality of these replacement brain cells, however, has not been conclusively determined. These discoveries have launched a paradigm shift in brain science.

A 2019 study published in *Cell Reports* reported that after surgeons removed one hemisphere in the brains of epileptic children, the remaining hemisphere rewired itself to restore normal functioning.

Peter Eriksson wrote, "Our study demonstrates that cell genesis occurs in human brains and that the human brain retains the potential for self-renewal throughout life."

Scientists believe that aerobic exercise has a beneficial effect on neurogenesis. Dr. Wendy A. Suzuki, Professor of Neural Science and Psychology at New York University, in her book *Healthy Brain, Happy Life* (2015), claims that aerobic exercise improves memory and learning. Cardiovascular activities like running, interval training, yoga, and cycling boost neurogenesis, burn calories, and reduce stress. Aerobic exercise, especially late in life, increases selected neurochemicals and glial cells that support neurogenesis. Conversely, a sedentary life style reduces neurogenesis.

In "The Impact of Diet on Adult Hippocampus," researchers Doris Stangl and Sandrine Thuret write, "One of the brain's structures associated with learning and memory, as well as mood, is the hippocampus. Interestingly, the hippocampus is one of the two structures in the adult brain where the formation of newborn neurons or neurogenesis persists."

To boost neurogenesis, you need a proper diet. Since 60 percent of the brain consists of fat, nutritionists recommend fueling your brain with proper vegetable and animal fats; eliminating refined sugars, processed foods, and saturated fats; reducing your caloric intake; increasing the time between meals; minimizing the intake of butter, cheese, and bacon; increasing the intake of walnuts, tuna, flax seeds, and blueberries; drinking green tea; and taking Omega-3 fish oils and turmeric (a spice with powerful antiarthritic and neurogenic properties).

Many studies confirm the adverse effects of sleep deprivation in the hippocampus, where neurogenesis primarily occurs. Two weeks or more of sleep deprivation inhibits neurogenesis. After you return to proper sleep, neurogenesis will proliferate brain cells normally. In addition to exercise, diet, and sleep, regular meditation also enhances neurogenesis.

Next time you drive your mother-in-law to The Furry Fiesta to buy cat food, wander over to the aquarium section and cast an appreciative nod to the zebra fish.

Instant Gratification

Mario craves instant gratification. When he snap-hooked two drives with his new $499 Wombat-580X Driver, he returned it to Dick's Sporting Goods. When he rimmed out two putts with his new $399 Holy Roller JCX Putter, he returned it to Golf Galaxy. When he uncrated his $655, special-order, chrome-trimmed, monogrammed, "Winnebago Tour Bag," he immediately filed a bogus $750 theft claim with Popko Insurance. However, Eddie Popko—*who knows a lot because he's seen a lot*—rejected Mario's claim.

Human brains are hard-wired for instant gratification. Decades ago, university psychologist Dr. Walter Mischel performed his famed "Marshmallow Experiment" to study self-control in children. Mischel presented preschoolers with a plate of marshmallows, then announced he was leaving the room. Before he left the room, however, he gave the children an option: They could receive *two* marshmallows in several minutes when he returned to the room. Or they could receive *one* marshmallow immediately by ringing a bell for him to return directly.

Mischel's experiment led to his *Hot and Cool Systems Theory* to explain why willpower fails or succeeds. Your cool-system, representing your planning and reflective brain, delays gratification in exchange for bigger rewards. Your hot-system, representing your impulsive and emotional brain, seeks immediate gratification in exchange for smaller rewards.

Your brain's medial orbital frontal cortex, responsible for making choices and anticipating rewards, has a decided preference for instant gratification. Psychologist Billi Gordon, in "Delayed Gratification: A Battle That Must be Won," asserts that when your brain anticipates an immediate reward, it releases dopamine, a powerful, pleasure-inducing neurochemical.

Neurochemicals feed your insatiable desire for instant results, quick fixes, silver bullets, and immediate success. Controlling your cravings for instant golfing success is akin to controlling your cravings for junk food, sweets, cigarettes, alcohol, sex, or drugs. Many golf instructors exploit your brain's addiction for quick fixes and silver bullets. Simply stated, golf addicts and drug addicts share a common neurochemical problem. Mischel's findings explain why golfers crave quick fixes.

In an era of instant gratification, you expect two-day shipping from Amazon, instantaneous downloads of movies, and immediate blind dates on E-Harmony. Smart phones, tablets, laptops, and the Internet fuel your brain's "hot-system."

Consequently, patience, willpower, and delayed gratification are in short supply. Without patience, however, you can't master complex skills. According to several sources, Mother Teresa said, "Without patience, we will learn less." If patience came easily, it wouldn't be a virtue.

Fitts and Posner, who introduced the three-stage learning model, maintain that the initial or cognitive stage of learning is characterized by recurring mistakes, setbacks, and failures. Thus, golfers accustomed to instant gratification tend to lose motivation during this difficult and humbling stage. Unless you delay gratification in exchange for long-term gains, you'll never improve.

Cognitive scientist Shahram Heshmat states, "We're hard-wired to want immediate payoffs, even if it's unwise." In his *Psychology Today* article, he posits that immediate gratification is predicated on a *time-based preference*. In other words, immediate outcomes take precedence over future outcomes.

He lists ten reasons that drive instant gratification: the reluctance to delay, the quest for rapid certainty, the need to satisfy impulses, the tendency to behave immaturely, the inability to plan properly, the pressure to address present needs, the spontaneity of the moment, the lack of emotional control, the craving for quick results, and the desire for immediate pleasure.

Unwary golfers—like sugar addicts—crave quick fixes. The word "addiction" is derived from the Latin term for "enslaved." In their article "How Addiction Highjacks the Brain," Harvard mental health experts identify the manifestations of all addictions: (1) a craving for more, (2) a loss of self-control, and (3) a wanton disregard for adverse consequences.

Dopamine—a neurotransmitter released from the brain's *nucleus accumbens* area located below your cerebral cortex—stimulates your brain's pleasure center. The more your addictions increase, the more dopamine you release. Addictions change your brain's structure and function. For many years, experts believed that only alcohol and drugs caused addiction. However, advances in neuroimaging demonstrate that other addictions—such as gambling, shopping, exercising, and quick fixes—affect your brain.

As swing mechanics becomes more technical, complex, and baffling, frustrated golfers take refuge in quick fixes. To tame this addiction, golfers must understand how their minds and brains function. If experts can hack your computer, they can hack your brain. Golfers addicted to quick fixes are easy prey for persuasive neuromarketers adept at manipulating your behavior.

Rx Golf

To understand the swing's complex nature, one must look beyond the system within which it is contained. All systems are multidisciplinary. All systems are nested within larger systems. Therefore, creative solutions to complex problems reside outside an existing system.

When you have a headache, you don't attach an aspirin to your forehead. You take a systemic approach by swallowing the aspirin so it dissolves in your stomach, gets absorbed in your bloodstream, and enters the nerves and muscles of your head and neck. When you snap-hook your ball into the woods, you don't attach lead weights on your hands to slow them down. You take a systemic approach by breathing deeply and relaxing your muscles to calm your ass down.

An analytical approach, which provides knowledge, tells you *how* aspirins and deep breathing function. A systemic approach, which provides explanations, tells you *why* aspirins and deep breathing function interactively and *why* you have a headache or aggressive swing in the first place. Let's compare drug prescriptions and swing prescriptions.

According to a recent *Consumer Reports* survey, an American adult takes an average of four prescription drugs. These prescription drugs are often unnecessary and dangerous.

In 2014, 1.3 million Americans were treated at ERs for adverse drug effects at a cost of more than $200 billion.

Pharmaceutical firms, which spend billions annually on marketing, have convinced patients and physicians there's a drug for every symptom. Studies indicate that 65 percent of all people who experience early symptoms—before they contact their physician—search the Internet for medical information even though they don't know what they're searching for. Catherine Roberts, in *Consumer Reports*, writes, ". . . the Internet is rife with unreliable health advice, which can result in false conclusions, unnecessary fear, and incorrect self-diagnosis."

Many patients who take four or more drugs prescribed by one or more physicians experience serious side effects that require additional drugs. Doctors who lack accurate information about a selected drug (e.g., Oxycontin) often fail to warn patients about its side effects. A *Consumer Report* study of 20 commonly prescribed drugs reviewed by Dr. Stephen Chen— USC's assistant dean of Pharmacy—revealed that 18 of these drugs caused serious problems. In fact, every drug introduced into your body's highly complex system causes minor, major, and unique side effects.

"Polypharmacy" refers to the practice of prescribing five or more medications by one or more physicians. Mary Brennan— an otherwise healthy 88-year-old woman—died in the hospital when her physicians prescribed 26 different medications. Golfers also experience "polypharmacy" when multiple swing prescriptions from different experts induce systemic side effects.

Dr. Victoria Sweet, in her book *Slow Medicine: The Way to Healing*, asserts that physicians practice medicine as if they were repairing machines. She writes, "Slow medicine means taking the time to get to the bottom of what's making people sick—including medications in some cases—and giving the body a chance to heal."

Drug prescriptions and swing prescriptions have much in common. Golfers adopt swing prescriptions—panaceas, cures, remedies, antidotes, and quick fixes from experts—through private lessons, group lessons, online lessons, YouTube videos, websites, chat rooms, blogs, books, and magazines. Golfers seeking fast medicine and quick fixes are susceptible to formulations that often exacerbate their problems.

Wonder drugs are special medications that provide patients with dramatic and positive relief for a host of illnesses and conditions. The golfing equivalent of wonder drugs are the *signature moves* in the swings of the game's best ball-strikers. For example, Moe Norman's "vertical drop and horizontal tug" was his signature move to shallow and reroute the club shaft in his downswing. Mike Austin's "compound pivot" was his signature move to shift his weight and rock his spine without moving his head. Lee Trevino's "chasing the ball down the line" was his signature move to lower his center of gravity and extend his right arm after impact. Signature moves are person-specific.

However, foolishly borrowing someone's wonder drug or signature move can be problematic. I'm not telling you to avoid signature moves. I'm telling you to test and employ the signature moves of great golfers whose personal parameters and swings are compatible with yours.

The latest *Physicians' Desk Reference*, weighing almost five pounds, provides physicians with detailed information on over 1,000 FDA-approved drugs. In the absence of a *Golfers' Desk Reference*, instructors and their pupils lack detailed information regarding hundreds of commonly prescribed swing remedies dispensed by qualified and unqualified practitioners.

Golfers exposed to hundreds of available, diverse, contradictory, anecdotal, untested, and unscientific prescriptions don't operate in an *information* vacuum. Rather, they operate in a *truth* vacuum. Commonly accepted swing prescriptions—such as keep your head down, torque your lower spine, relax your muscles, and loosen your grip—are based on myths, falsehoods, half-truths, contradictions, misconceptions, and fallacies.

Golfers using ill-advised swing therapies often incur serious injuries. In "Golf Injuries: An Overview" (in *Sports Medicine*), G. Thériault and P. Lachance claim that golf's most common injuries to the lower back, shoulders, wrists, and elbows can be prevented by ". . . the adjustment of an individual's golf swing to meet their physical capacities and limitations through properly supervised golf lessons."

Tiger Woods, under the supervision of distinguished coaches including two with graduate degrees in biomechanics and kinesiology, has undergone four back operations and four knee operations. Under expert supervision, Tiger has also injured his neck, left arm, left leg, and elbows. Tiger Woods *and* his celebrated coaches—Butch Harmon, Hank Haney, Sean Foley, and Chris Como—deserve both credit and blame for his triumphs, failures, and injuries.

Tiger has done serious damage to his back and knees by rotating through his lumbar spine and employing a "squat-jump," as his coaches prescribed. Butch Harmon advised Tiger to "snap" his left knee on impact to increase power, clubhead speed, and distance. Consequently, Tiger underwent ACL repair and arthroscopy in 2008 caused by years of snapping his left knee at impact.

To prevent further knee damage, Tiger eliminated his knee snap. To compensate for his resultant loss of power, Tiger's coaches advised him to rotate excessively through his hips and back. As a result, Tiger now suffers from chronic back pain caused by a pinched nerve and a bulging disc. To gain more direction control, Tiger's coaches reduced his distance by prescribing a more compact swing. Ironically, Tiger's more compact swing, which induced a quicker and more aggressive transition, lacked both direction control and distance. After spinal fusion on his lower back in late 2016, Tiger Woods parted company with swing coach Chris Como.

Moreover, Tiger's personal trainers, who bulked up his upper arms and chest, prescribed the wrong fitness regimen. Instead of making Tiger's limbs long, slim, wiry, and free-wheeling for better leverage and less inertia, his fitness coaches made his chest and arms thicker, slower, and more muscular. Recently, Tiger emptied his "medicine cabinet" of all swing prescriptions except for putting prescriptions.

Only 43.5 percent of the information on *medical* websites, according to several studies, is accurate and relevant. Unfortunately, no studies have assessed the accuracy and relevance of information on *golf* websites.

I'm not telling you to stop searching websites for swing prescriptions. I'm saying you must be *digitally literate and self-scrutinizing* to search golf websites. You need knowledge to use knowledge. Accessing accurate and relevant information in the electronic jungle is a daunting endeavor.

In his *New York Times* article "How the Internet is Losing Our Grip on the Truth," Farhad Manjoo writes, "Psychologists and other social scientists have repeatedly shown that when confronted with diverse information choices, people rarely act like rational, civic-minded automatons. Instead, we are roiled by preconceptions and biases, and we usually do what feels easiest—we gorge on information that confirms our ideas and we shun what does not."

Since the advent of the World Wide Web in 1989, experts have posted many valuable swing prescriptions. This doesn't mean that swing prescriptions introduced before 1989 are irrelevant or obsolete. Frankly, the imperishable swing prescriptions introduced decades ago by Bobby Jones, Ernest Jones, Joe Dante, and many others still abide.

The main problem among golfers searching for accurate and relevant swing prescriptions is "over-choice"—Alvin Toffler's term in *Future Shock* (1970) that denotes the phenomenon of choosing from a bewildering number of options.

Autodidacts

Sam Snead won a record 82 professional tournaments (presently in a tie with Tiger Woods). He taught himself a world-class golf swing by hitting rocks in the fields of Hot Springs, Virginia. Snead said, "I didn't take lessons since I didn't have anybody to work with. I just tried to make it as simple as possible. If you keep it simple, you make it look easy. I just wanted a swing that would hold up."

Snead built his classic swing on one organizing principle or mobilizing idea: *"Move everything together."* To move everything together, Snead used a forward press initiated by his hands. Snead's forward press—his chicken soup remedy for his ailing golf swing—earned him fame and fortune. Snead demonstrates that a championship swing can be self-taught.

Self-taught, self-educated, and self-learning individuals like Sam Snead are called *autodidacts*. In Ancient Greek *autos* means "self" and *didaktos* means "taught." Famous autodidacts, such as Leonardo da Vinci, Galileo, Ben Franklin, Abe Lincoln, Charles Darwin, Nikola Tesla, Thomas Edison, the Wright Brothers, Buckminster Fuller, Frank Lloyd Wright, Henry Ford, and Ernest Hemingway, have changed the world.

The best way to learn something is to have someone teach it to you is an *instructional myth*. How did you learn to talk, walk, ride a bike, or jump over puddles? You may have used outside resources, but essentially you taught yourself.

As a child you taught yourself to speak your native language. And no instructor, Berlitz tape, or Rosetta Stone program can teach you to speak a second language better than you can speak your native language.

Have you ever taught a group of people a subject that you previously knew nothing about? If so, who learned more—you or your students? Teaching yourself and teaching others is a boon to learning. Being taught is an obstruction to learning. *Learning how to learn* and *learning how to motivate yourself to learn* are the most important things to learn.

Motivation is the key to learning. Intrinsically motivated learners solve problems, achieve goals, and acquire new skills because it's personally satisfying. Extrinsically motivated learners solve problems, achieve goals, and acquire new skills to earn rewards and avoid punishment.

Neuroscientists, using modern neural-imaging techniques, are now equipped to study the cognitive processes of learning, memory, and motivation. Psychologists Stefano Di Domenico and Richard Ryan attribute the passionate pursuit of intrinsic motivation among self-learners to elevated levels of dopamine in their brain's pleasure-center. In sum, dopamine fuels the desire of self-learners to seek the intrinsic rewards associated with mastering skills and achieving breakthroughs.

Many successful golfers—including Moe Norman, Mike Austin, Calvin Peete, Lee Trevino, Bubba Watson, J.B. Holmes, Jim Herman, and Jim Furyk—taught themselves the golf swing.

Lee Trevino said, "The greatest thing about being self-taught is that you can correct yourself on the course." When self-learners under pressure lose their swing, they ask themselves, "How can I restore my swing's natural rhythm?" When taught-learners under pressure lose their swing, they ask themselves, "How did my instructor solve this problem?" Akin to tightrope walkers, golfers must *feel*—not *think*—their way across the high wire.

To simplify complex swing mechanics, self-taught golfers rely on unique *master-controls* congealed into simple thoughts, analogies, and mantras. Bubba Watson, who never took a lesson, learned his swing by curving whiffle balls around trees in his backyard and hitting lobs shots over furniture in his living room. Watson claims that squaring up the clubface at impact is his primary swing-thought.

In "Do It Yourself: Swings" (*Golf Digest*), Bubba Watson states, "All you need to worry about is three feet of the swing from 5 o'clock to 7 o'clock [for right-handed golfers] right before and at impact." The common denominator in all efficient swings is the position of the clubface as it enters and exits the impact zone. When Bubba views videos of his swing, he focuses on his impact position. To enhance your self-learning, film your swing to make adjustments and detect mistakes (e.g., releasing the club too early or too late).

In 2013, Dick's Sporting Goods ran a television commercial showing a montage of golf swings from various men, women, and children. Against a musical background, Arnold Palmer softly spoke the following words: "Swing your own swing. Not some idea of a swing. Not a swing you saw on television. Not a swing you wish you had. No . . . Swing your swing." The commercial ended with Palmer swinging a club during his prime and saying, "I know I did."

Palmer was telling golfers to complement formalized instruction with self-discovery. He wanted golfers to find their own swings by adhering to self-confirmed principles—not by borrowing the swings of others to mimic their rigid and prescribed body movements and club positions.

Self-learning—not expert instruction—revolutionized my swing. When I studied videos of Bubba Watson, for example,

I observed how he inverted and reversed (i.e., switched the orientation) of the butt end and clubhead 180-degrees in his backswing and downswing. He swung the butt end in a tilted circle, vertically raised and lowered his arms, twirled his wrist axles, and rotated his forearms and shoulder joints. Inverting and reversing the club while you're pivoting is akin to wielding a sabre to slash at a ball on the ground. When I inverted and reversed the orientation of the butt end and clubhead in my backswing and downswing—primarily by twirling my wrist axles—I remained on plane and increased my swing speed.

Teacher-bound golfers take heed. In 1999, Dr. Sugata Mitra, a professor of Educational Technology, conducted a fascinating experiment to study the learning habits of children who never used a computer. Mitra's "Hole in the Wall" experiment consisted of an Internet-equipped computer and a video camera installed in the cavity of a wall separating his research lab from a busy street in a New Delhi slum. To Mitra's amazement, the children quickly taught themselves to turn on the computer, use the keyboard, surf the Internet in a foreign language, download movies, play games, and draw pictures using Microsoft Paint.

Clutter

Recently you helped Vinnie unclutter his attic. After you removed 19 contractor bags loaded with old clothes and useless junk, you spotted a large object covered in a blanket. When you removed the blanket, you couldn't believe your eyes. It was a life-size, fiberglass pig that weighed probably 60 pounds.

When Vinnie saw you examining the pig, he said, "It's a lawn ornament. Leave it. It's staying!" Apparently, a former girlfriend who worked at the Iowa State Fair gave it to Vinnie 27 years ago as a birthday gift. Although Vinnie cherishes the pig, his wife won't allow him to put on the lawn. Getting rid of old stuff is never easy.

Golfers must also unclutter their "attic" of myths, half-truths, falsehoods and illusions. When old knowledge interferes with your brain's ability to process new knowledge, you stop learning. Discarding obsolete, outdated, and useless knowledge is akin to removing junk from your attic. However, you don't need to make physical space in your brain for new ideas. You need to overwrite old neural pathways with new ones.

Unlearning and *relearning* are interrelated. Before you can build and strengthen new neural connections, you must break down old ones. Deleting old knowledge, habits, and skills is called "synaptic pruning." Researchers are trying to understand exactly how neurons facilitate learning by making new synaptic connections.

When you sleep, your brain cells shrink by 60 percent, thereby allowing it to remove useless connections. When you're tired, your brain seems full. When you wake up refreshed and invigorated, your brain seems empty. That's because certain "trash-collecting" neurons (i.e., microglial cells) unclutter your brain when you're asleep.

How do you replace defunct notions, habits, and practices with new and relevant ones? First, you must prove that your existing beliefs and practices don't work by questioning your assumptions and playing devil's advocate. If your existing swing notions don't work, figure out why. Second, broaden your information base by exploring fresh and unconventional resources. For example, if you've been using Leadbetter's analytical approach, consider Ernest Jones's holistic approach. Third, abandon your limitations and escape your cognitive prison. For example, empty your "mental filing cabinet" filled with dated information regarding swing plane, spinal tilt, weight shift, wrist action, etc.

Actually purge your attic, basement, and garage of *material clutter* of useless putters, drivers, golf bags, golf shoes, and training aids. Then purge your brain of *mental clutter* consisting of failed methodologies, notions, and practices. Removing physical and mental clutter will enhance your joy and productivity. The residue of physical and mental clutter represents unfinished business, unsolved problems, previous struggles, and dashed hopes. Retain what's useful and dump the rest.

Again, you can't unclutter your brain as if it were an attic. You can't erase existing neural pathways. Here are a few suggestions to superimpose new neural pathways over old ones.

First, *change your mindset.* To learn proper swing mechanics, adopt a fresh outlook. Don't transfer skill sets from tennis or baseball to golf. Tennis rackets, baseball bats, and golf clubs—with different hitting surfaces, weights, and grips—have their own specific muscle-sequencing patterns.

Applying neural pathways from your baseball swing to your golf swing doesn't work. Therefore, establish new neural pathways. Stop trying to define and understand the golf paradigm—an inherently unique and complex movement—based on a baseball paradigm. Stop swinging a baseball bat on the golf course.

Second, *open your mind.* Remain available to new beliefs and approaches. If you surround yourself with others who share similar beliefs and practices, you won't entertain new ideas. You won't get what you never had if you don't do what you've never done.

Amass new knowledge. Glean information from all directions. When Caesar's troops accidentally burned The Library of Alexandria in 42 BC, new knowledge became necessary. When a forest fire bursts the shells of seedlings, new and healthy trees will emerge.

Third, *nurture self-awareness.* Self-reflection—providing keen insights for growth—helps you realize you've been brainwashed. Don't wait for a golf messiah to put your game in order. Put yourself in order. Thinking, feeling, and doing comprise your makeup. Change one, and the others will follow.

In *Walden*, Henry David Thoreau describes his experience of living alone in a small cabin in the woods for two years, two months, and two days between 1845 and 1847. When he had worn a path through the woods, he knew it was time to leave. His feet and brain needed new pathways.

Neuroplasticity allows you to create new pathways. You can't remove existing neural pathways and old memories in the same way you remove attic clutter. But you can overwrite old neural pathways with new ones. Your neurological attic has unlimited storage space. Get busy deciding what new neural pathways and fresh memory traces you want to store up there.

Cognitive Dissonance

Consider the innumerable, contradictory, and diverse swing paradigms, methodologies, instructors, equipment choices, training devices, videos, books, and articles at your disposal. To know what's relevant, accurate, and useful, you must sharpen your critical thinking skills.

To jump-start your improvement, recognize and alter your delusional thinking and moronic habits. Accept the fact that your poor swing, high scores, and erratic play flow from fuzzy thinking.

Most complex swing methodologies containing eight "simple" positions or seven "easy" steps are inherently flawed. The human brain isn't hard-wired to execute a complex sequence of conscious, neuromuscular commands in a span of 1.4 seconds. Get real. If your swing paradigm can't be easily stored and readily retrieved from your subconscious, adopt one that can be. Adopt a simple—not a simplistic—swing paradigm.

Mastering the golf swing—an unfamiliar, unnatural, counterintuitive movement—is a daunting task. Thus, be prepared to generate new brain cells and make new synaptic connections. Use your mind to change your brain in order to change your movement patterns.

Sports psychologists assert that golfers have one of the flattest learning curves and slowest improvement rates among all athletes. Unlike weight lifters, cyclists, and martial arts practitioners, golfers tend to enjoy a short spurt of initial improvement, then languish for decades. Why?

"The Cognitive Dissonance Theory" holds that people ignore stressful information that contradicts their existing beliefs. In sum, performance anxiety or stress shuts down your capacity to think logically when you're confronted with refutations, counterevidence, and opposing beliefs.

Steven Hoffman, a research sociologist, published an interesting study on cognitive dissonance. He writes, "Rather than search rationally for information that either confirms or disconfirms a particular belief, people actually seek out information that confirms what they already believe." Does this sound familiar?

Hoffman asserts that zero-growth learners ignore contrary information, adopt half-ass rationalizations, accept false information, and cling to erroneous ideas and failed practices.

Hoffman calls this backward chain of reasoning "inferred justification." If you're convinced that purchasing a new $500 driver or attending "The Miracle Golf Academy" for one week following your 75th birthday will transform your golf game, you're employing "inferred justification." Essentially, you're justifying and embracing preexisting and delusional beliefs.

Experiencing cognitive dissonance, however, isn't the problem. The problem is *ignoring* cognitive dissonance and clinging to delusional thinking and self-destructive practices.

Cognitive dissonance, the residue of failed expectations, arises when a lengthy practice session, professional lesson, promising methodology, expensive equipment change, or new training aid doesn't pan out.

Suppose you spend $500 on a new driver. Totally ignoring your bad back, poor diet, and lousy swing, you're nonetheless convinced this new club will produce miracles. You've marveled at how Carmine's new driver transformed his game.

However, what happens when your new driver club doesn't produce miracles? What happens when your new driver makes things worse? You get pissed, disillusioned, and disgusted. You can't think straight. You wasted $500 (plus $20.95 for two-day shipping) on a useless driver.

Cognitive dissonance swirls around your brain like a banshee on rollerblades. To allay cognitive dissonance, you suspend critical thinking, ignore your failures, and develop "situation blindness."

Despite the glowing endorsements and promises associated with your driver, the damn thing doesn't work. Nonetheless, you keep it in your bag, ignore your dismal drives, maintain your delusional thinking, and cling to your failed beliefs.

Noted psychologist Leon Festinger offers some interesting insights on delusional thinking. He studied why people ignore facts, discredit contrary information, and confirm their biases. If your game is languishing, you may find the results interesting.

In a book he coauthored with Henry Riecken and Stanley Schachter titled *When Prophecy Fails* (1956), Festinger recounts his classic study of cognitive dissonance. Festinger infiltrated a religious cult whose members believed that the Earth would end on a specified time and date. Cult members assembled at a designated location to await the catastrophe. However, nothing happened. The Earth didn't explode. Damn it. No Armageddon!

The catastrophic moment came and went. It's like your "nothing-happened-moment" on the driving range when your $500 driver didn't work. Your drives still stink. How can this be?

Festinger relates how these delusional cult members, who donated their entire life savings to their oddball leaders, quelled their cognitive dissonance by ignoring what just happened.

Cult leaders, employing "inferred justification," claimed that benevolent Martians interceded at the last moment to spare the Earth from destruction. Unable to face the facts, cult members took refuge in ignorance, delusion, and rationalization. They blamed aliens. Failed golfers, deluded by golf's cult of experts, also employ "inferred justification."

Festinger reported that cult membership actually increased following their failed prediction. Embracing the cult's Martian theory, hundreds of new members signed up.

Daryl Bem, a social psychologist, has a different view of why people cling to delusions. In his book *Self-Perception Theory*, Bem claims that people think and behave irrationally, not to allay cognitive dissonance, but to bolster their pride, ego, and self-esteem. Egotistical people can't admit their failures and drop their pretensions. In his experiment, Bem assigned test participants a variety of dreadfully boring tasks. He then asked participants, "Did you find these tasks interesting?"

Test participants, contrary to their beliefs, claimed that these boring tasks were interesting for two reasons: (1) because so-called authorities said the tasks were interesting and (2) because researchers paid selected subjects $20 to say the tasks were interesting.

In brief, endorsements and monetary rewards induce delusional thinking. People, swayed by their egos, are often deluded by lofty testimonials and rewards.

Golfers, take heed. The more money you spend on clubs, methodologies, videos, training aids, and books endorsed by acclaimed experts, the more you'll ignore your dismal results, failed practices, and delusional thinking.

The implications of Bem's research are relevant for golfers. You will readily discard your knockoff $60 driver and no-name $15 putter. Yet you'll stubbornly cling to your equally useless $500 driver and $350 putter. In sum, money and acclaim drive delusional thinking.

Psychologist Jack Brehem conducted a related experiment. Brehem asked his subjects to rate various small kitchen appliances. Then Brehem presented his participants with a specific appliance as a thank-you gift. When Brehem asked his subjects to rate their thank-you gifts, they enhanced their previous ratings. Brehem asserts that people tend to justify, confirm, and reinforce—not challenge, doubt, and modify—their pre-existing thinking. In short, people tend to reinforce rather than challenge their existing beliefs.

Cognitive dissonance and ego-induced delusional thinking reinforce preexisting beliefs, block contradictory evidence, and foster stagnation.

One of the biggest obstacles to growth is delusional thinking. The longer you delude yourself, the longer you'll stagnate. To enhance your cognitive skills, focus on what you're thinking and why you're thinking it. "Know thyself."

No Sacred Cows

In golf, there are no pat answers, universal fixes, or immediate panaceas. Nonetheless, golfers continue to embrace shortcuts and untested methodologies that provide wishful thinking.

Skepticism is a question mark. Certainty is an exclamation point. To improve your game, punctuate your golf journey with question marks. Skepticism invites critical thinking and establishes validity. If you refuse to interrogate sources and authorities, you're an easy prey for charlatans and false prophets.

Skepticism, a valuable mindset, forms the foundation for continuous learning and growth. Aristotle said, "It is the mark of an educated mind to entertain a thought without accepting it." To learn the golf swing, examine multiple instructors, principles, practices, theories, methodologies, and approaches from various sources. Trade certainty for doubt.

When golfers have no answers to certain problems, they're *ignorant*. When they have hunches about certain answers, they're *uncertain*. When they reach *certainty*—the omega point—they'll *stagnate*. When it comes to learning, unlearning, and relearning, there's no finish line.

For centuries, golf experts have made assertions—some untrue, some partially true—about the workings of the golf swing. Therefore, beware of sacred cows. Experts can't transfer what they don't possess.

Great thinkers advance their knowledge through skepticism. A skeptical mindset, the great liberator, lets you process information critically and independently. Remaining skeptical lets you open new doors, travel fresh paths, and entertain alternatives.

Most golfers are imprisoned by flawed beliefs and shaky methodologies. If learning to play golf—like learning to ride a bike—were simple, intuitive, and accessible, golfers would thrive. However, that's not the case. Thus, growth-minded golfers must revolutionize their thinking and question conventional approaches. However, challenging golf's sacred cows—immune from questioning and criticism—is difficult for many reasons.

Neuroscientists claim that conformity—the tendency to embrace consensual opinions—is hard-wired into our brains. Researcher Vasily Klucharev used magnetic resonance imaging to measure brain activity. Whenever you take a risk, your brain sends two alerts: *This is a mistake* and *This will end badly*.

Simply put, your brain is hard-wired for conformity and acceptance—not risk and skepticism. Conformity and acceptance—like a large electric blanket—are very comforting. Researchers refer to the emotional cost of defying conformity as "the pain of independence."

Researchers theorize that conformity flows from (1) our fear of being different and (2) our uncertainty about what we're doing. In his book *Iconoclast: A Neuroscientist Reveals How to Think Differently* (2008), Dr. Gregory Berns writes, "One reason behind conformity is that, in terms of human evolution, going against the group is not beneficial to survival. There is a tremendous survival advantage to being in a community. Our brains are exquisitely tuned to what other people think about us, aligning our judgments to fit in with the group."

When Berns conducted experiments in which a test subject was placed with a group of four actors, he found that his test subjects subordinated their opinions to suit the group's prepared wrong answers over 40 percent of the time. In brief, it's easier and safer to agree than disagree.

To actualize growth, remain skeptical and open. Think critically and independently. Monitor and test thoroughly. Your swing beliefs dictate your performance and constitute your game.

Most PGA instructors, espousing relatively similar guidelines, principles, and methods, are peas in a pod. Admittedly, each instructor is unique. However, most PGA instructors share similar backgrounds, training, and experience; employ similar anecdotal evidence; reference similar data; and draw similar conclusions.

PGA instructors are akin to bicycles. There are roughly twenty-two different types of bicycles that have two wheels and function in similar fashion. Similarly, there many PGA instructors and amateur instructors who function in similar fashion. Therefore, choose the best one for you.

I'm not telling you to doubt, reject, or dismiss popular advice. I'm telling you to exercise skepticism. Read omnivorously. Investigate broadly. Doubt intelligently. If you're skeptical, you're standing in the right place.

Resist the temptation to adopt simple formulas. You are what you settle for. When someone offers you a quick, easy, and simplistic solution to your golf problems, humble yourself. Choose instead the less satisfying but far healthier response: "I don't know about that." Doubt is two parts suspicion and one part anticipation.

Danish physicist Neils Bohr said, "The opposite of a correct statement is a false statement. But the opposite of a profound truth may well be another profound truth." The truth is never easy.

Bamboozled

Golfers overly confident in their beliefs get bamboozled. Don't let your confidence outweigh your intelligence. *Golf contrarians* look deeply, think creatively, ask probing questions, and drink from many wells. Conversely, *golf conformists* look superficially, think narrowly, ask few questions, and drink from only one or two wells.

History reminds us to take expert advice with a grain of salt. Most CIA analysts never anticipated the sudden dissolution of the USSR! Most Wall Street financiers never predicted the collapse of the nation's largest investment firms! Most Pentagon experts never imagined a multitrillion-dollar fiasco in Iraq and Afghanistan. Simply put, highly credentialed experts are often dead wrong.

Several key psychological studies reveal how people, including the most intelligent and educated, get bamboozled. Researchers call this phenomenon "The Dr. Fox Effect." In a series of famous experiments, researchers employed a fictional authority, Dr. Myron L. Fox, played by a professional actor. Researchers introduced Dr. Fox to an audience of professional educators. Dr. Fox delivered a specious lecture applying mathematical game theory to physical education classes. It was a total hoax!

Dr. Fox lectured enthusiastically, humorously, and authoritatively. However, Dr. Fox was a fraud. Researchers then asked audience members to evaluate the lecture. The results were astonishing!

According to questionnaires, the audience was overwhelmingly impressed with Dr. Fox's expertise. In fact, one educator complained that the lecture was "too intellectual." Bottom line: Look beyond your instructors' impressive credentials, lofty status, authoritative tone, and personal assurances before you accept their advice.

Phillip Tetlock, author of *Expert Political Judgment* (2005), studied 82,000 political predictions by 284 so-called experts. When Tetlock tracked how their predictions panned out, he discovered that their predictions were nothing more than random guesses! Furthermore, Tetlock discovered that the most famous experts make the worst predictions! Conversely, less famous experts make the best predictions.

Tetlock based his findings on Sir Isaiah Berlin's famous distinction between the thinking styles of *hedgehogs* and *foxes*. Famous experts or *hedgehogs* held strong biases, rigid convictions, and narrow world views. Obscure experts or *foxes* were more cautious, inquisitive, pragmatic, skeptical, and open-minded. The *foxes* adjusted their views, exercised self-doubt, and embraced complexity and nuance.

Bottom line: Look beyond a golf instructor's glitter and fame. Anonymous and intelligent amateurs on YouTube often purvey the most valuable advice.

Furthermore, expert advice is often highly overrated. In one experiment, researchers concluded that clinical psychologists did no better than their secretaries in diagnosing the conditions of selected patients. Next time your shrink is booked, consult a clerk at Ace Hardware.

Critically assess all advice. Einstein stated, "Unthinking respect for authority is the greatest enemy of truth."

In *Anti-Intellectualism in American Life* (1963), Richard Hofstadter wrote, "... the complexity of modern life has steadily whittled away the functions the ordinary citizen can intelligently and competently perform for himself." Since critical thinking is no longer a core element in the education system, according to Hofstadter, one must take personal responsibility for what one thinks and why one thinks it. For needy and lazy golfers, this is a most unsettling revelation.

The "curate's egg"—a popular British idiom—denotes something that's not entirely satisfactory. The term can be traced to a George du Maurier cartoon published in *Punch* magazine in 1895. A nervous curate, or junior cleric, is eating a spoiled egg at the bishop's table. When the bishop expresses concern that the egg is bad, the curate, who wishes not to offend, says, "Oh, my Lord, I assure you that parts of it are excellent." The "curate's egg" allusion denotes something that contains both good parts and bad parts. This term applies to modern golf instruction. Accept advice selectively, since most methodologies have good and bad parts.

Yale researchers found that white rats repeatedly beat psychology undergraduates in discovering optimal routes for getting food dropped into a maze. Rats in a race for food outperformed Ivy League students who tended to overanalyze things. Learn a lesson from the rats in Yale's psychology laboratory: Find your own optimal route to the cheese!

Beware of gurus who act as if their brain were far smarter than anyone else's. Become your own guru by experiencing the mystery of golf deepened by your own contact with reality.

Along my golf journey, I learned to question expert advice. Often the advice they offered didn't match the words they were preaching and the things they were doing.

I'm not telling you to avoid expert advice. I'm telling you to filter expert advice. Don't blindly accept advice from Jordan

Speith, Justin Rose, or Jason Day or their mentors. You're not Jordan, Justin, or Jason. You're *you!*

When you're working with experts, *stop asking them to solve your problems* and *start asking them to help you understand the swing as a highly complex, tightly coupled system.*

My heroes are self-made and self-taught individuals like Robinson Crusoe, who landed on a deserted island with few resources and improved his quality of life all by himself. Self-learning is the path to competency.

Big Data

When Vinnie learned that his favorite Tour pro used swing diagnostics to win The Masters, he spent $1,200 on Pro-Tech's "Big Data Package" consisting of three hourly sessions. (Vinnie used the money from his tax refund without telling his wife.)

Intoxicated after reading Pro-Tech's brochure, Vinnie coveted Golf's Holy Grail. He learned the 48 crucial body and club positions of elite golfers. Pro-Tech uses 18 body sensors to provide 3-D swing diagnostics and a launch monitor to record ballistics.

Vinnie said, "It's about time I got all my shit in one sock." However, things didn't pan out. Vinnie, who flunked high school math, hates numbers. His $1,200 golf investment transformed him from a 22 handicap to a 28 handicap. Attaining your bliss and stalking your bliss are two different things.

Today, many PGA Tour pros, coaches, and instructors diagnose swings with expensive and sophisticated analyzers and simulators that cost between $60,000 and $4,000, such as Full Swing S2, Full Swing S8, X-Golf, Golf Blaster, HD Golf, P3 Pro Swing, TruTrack, Par2Pro, and TrackMan.

Many simulators are equipped with internal HD cameras that can record 2,300 frames per second and dual radar systems that can make 6,000 calculations per second. Simulators provide precise body, club, and ball metrics for dozens of positions during the swing.

Simulators furnish precise data regarding weight transfer, shoulder tilt, hip sway, pelvis rotation, ball speed, club speed, launch angle, smash factor, clubface angle, ball spin axis, ball spin rate, landing distance, carry distance, etc. Moreover, simulators can compare your swing parameters frame by frame with those of Tour pros.

The TrackMan website states, "We track the full trajectory of any shot, from 6-foot pitches to 400-yard drives, pinpointing the landing position with an accuracy of less than 1 foot at 100 yards. We also display the shot's 3D trajectory together with 26 impact and ball flight parameters in real time (data is delivered within 1 second)."

To satisfy the growing demand for swing diagnostics, instructors are buying expensive equipment housed in Golf Learning Centers that resemble MRI facilities staffed by technicians in white lab coats. However, many swing diagnostic centers, boasting 96 percent success rates, offer no guarantees and charge approximately $200 per hour or almost triple what club pros charge.

When you get plugged into a diagnostic system, you hit practice balls to a simulated fairway or green. Based on body movements, club positions, and ball flight, the computer downloads images and data to supply you with corrective measures. However, many clients complain that their swing technicians lack the expertise and communications skills to teach them what they need to learn.

Whether swing diagnostics foster lasting and measurable improvement is an open question. Anecdotal evidence suggests that big data pays the highest dividends among analytical thinkers and visual learners (compared to systemic thinkers and kinesthetic learners). Unfortunately, most diagnostic programs are too expensive for the average golfer.

In the collective writings of Ernest Jones, Bobby Jones, Ben Hogan, Byron Nelson, and Sam Snead, the word *data* never appears. Today's data-driven *analytical* model of teaching and learning—in which body and club positions are minutely dissected—is antithetical to yesterday's kinesthetic or holistic model.

Diagnostic data are only useful if you can analyze and interpret it. To process swing analytics, you must be *data-literate*. In brief, you must be able to extract useful information from data the way literate people extract useful information from the written word.

In his TED Talk titled "The Age of Data Literacy," Uldis Leiterts states that data analysis, requiring knowledge of mathematics and statistics, has become so sophisticated and specialized that corporations now hire *Chief Data Officers* with advanced analytical skills to interpret the results.

According to Leiterts, a data-literate person must know which data are appropriate for a particular purpose, how to interpret data visualizations (e.g., screen shots, graphs, and charts), how to think critically about data-driven information, how to recognize misleading data, and how to communicate data clearly to others. If you and your golf technician are not data-literate, you're screwed.

Furthermore, to interpret swing data accurately, you must be able to distinguish *correlation* from *causation*. Correlation denotes the unrelated connection between variables. Illogically connecting your poor round to that hideous brown-and-pink-striped IZOD shirt your mother-in-law gave you is an example of correlation.

Causation denotes a direct, logical, and scientific connection between variables. Logically connecting your poor play to added grip pressure and a quicker backswing is an example of causation.

Here's the rub. Determining direct, logical, and scientific causal relationships among highly complex and elusive movements involving hundreds of joints, muscles, and bones during a 1.4-second interval is a daunting task. How do you establish causation in a golf swing employing innumerable, nuanced, and invisible anatomical forces and pressures? Without expert and enlightened analysis, swing data are useless.

In their article "Good Data Won't Guarantee Good Decisions" (*Harvard Business Review*), Shvetank Shah, Andrew Horne, and Jaime Capellá identify three different types of data-based decision-makers: (1) Unquestioning Empiricists, (2) Visceral Decision Makers, and (3) Informed Skeptics.

Unquestioning Empiricists trust analysis over judgment. Visceral Decision Makers rely exclusively on their gut. Informed Skeptics, who are best equipped to make good decisions, can analyze data, listen intently, weigh opinions, and dissent intelligently. Which one are you?

Shah, Horne, and Capellá offer a succinct warning to decision-makers. "At this very moment, there's an odds-on chance that someone in your organization is making a poor decision on the basis of information that was enormously expensive to collect."

Are you making poor swing decisions based on expensive, misleading, complicated, and technical data beyond your ken?

I'm not saying that analytical data are unreliable and irrelevant. I'm saying you must be *data-literate*. In sum, you must be able to use and interpret diverse data sets, employ causal thinking, solve complex problems, and make sound decisions. Unfortunately, most failed golfers lack these critical skills. Therefore, determine whether you and your swing technician are capable of harvesting expensive and complex swing data. Why pursue useless data?

Scott Gnau, in "Putting Big Data in Context" (*Wired*), warns readers about an overreliance on big data. Gnau asserts that you should base your decisions not only on data analytics, but also on human intuition. He writes, "There is a great debate today in machine learning circles about the nature of the human brain, and whether our minds can be reduced to a system of symbolic representations that can be ultimately replicated by machines. . . . Software cannot replicate human imagination, intuition and consciousness. Whatever the case, it is clear that over-reliance on data can be misleading."

The Big Data Approach, an evolutionary step in analytical thinking, represents a new mode of golf teaching and learning. To optimize the benefits of big data, consider integrating not only (1) statistical information and intuition, but also (2) analytical thinking (i.e., dissecting the swinging motion) and holistic thinking (i.e., unifying the swinging motion). An overdependence on big data—obfuscation by complexity—may erode your intuition, creativity, and imagination.

Observational Learning

You have learned a lot by observing others, especially your mother-in-law. You have never run out of milk ever since you observed your mother-in-law add 12 Milk of Magnesia tablets, a cup of water, and some cornflakes into her cereal bowl. By observing the habits of others, you learn *what to do* and w*hat not to do.*

Observational learning teaches you which behaviors to imitate and which ones to avoid. *Imitative* learning, a more empathetic and intense form of observational learning, teaches you to replicate the sensations and movements of others.

When you passively watch a video of Ben Hogan's swing, for example, you're employing *observational* learning. However, when you internalize and replicate Hogan's movements, you're employing *imitative* learning.

Eighty percent of all sensory information is visual. Observational skills, often taken for granted, are most important for making sense of your environment and enhancing your performance. Observational deficits create performance deficits.

Neurologists claim that observational learning takes place in the brain's "Action Observation Network" (AON), where neurons fire when you observe or perform movements.

Dr. Scott Grafton, using MRI imaging, studied the brain's AON area among participants learning complicated dance steps. In his paper "What Can Dance Teach Us About Learning?" Grafton writes, "Discovery of the AON has revitalized interest in motor simulation theory, which holds that we use our own motor memories to figure out what other people are doing. When we watch a video of a dancer, motor areas of the brain might activate automatically and unconsciously—even though our bodies are not actually moving—to find familiar patterns that we can use to interpret what we are watching. In other words, some sort of resonance takes place between the circuits for observing and for doing. If this is true, the AON should be more active when we observe actions that are physically familiar than it is when we observe unfamiliar actions."

When swing movements get too complicated, verbal instructions become impractical. Written or spoken instructions employing imprecise, ambiguous, misinterpreted, and vague words to teach precise movements are less effective than visual images.

When you encounter discrepancies between what instructors are saying and what they're doing, concentrate primarily on what they're doing. In other words, use observational, not auditory learning as your default mode. Your AON circuitry is more active when you're observing and less active when you're listening.

Research findings confirm that you acquire motor skills more rapidly and precisely when you model *live* movements rather than *recorded* movements. Therefore, adapt the movements of live models to build your swing.

Researchers have shown that the brain's AON regions respond when you're observing and performing. In sum, you can learn positive movement patterns—and avoid negative movement patterns—not only through *passive* observation, but also through *active* participation. Fire up those AON neurons.

Let your observational skills collude, not conflict, with your learning habits.

When I viewed slow-motion videos of Mike Austin's swing to learn how he moved his right elbow, I achieved one of my biggest breakthroughs in over three decades.

The Grass Whip

Golfers who employ defunct methodologies are akin to medieval patients who use blood-sucking leeches to cure diseases.

Many unscientific and unfounded conventional approaches, like leeches, are sucking dry your precious time, effort, and money.

To achieve *hands-down-I-am-not-fooling-around* improvement, explore unconventional approaches. Find new, simple approaches to improve your skills.

When you first learned to fly a kite, did you clutter your head with aeronautical principles and anatomical positions? Or did you employ simple instructions, natural instincts, and kinesthetic sensations? Moreover, once you learned basic kite flying, did you need ongoing lessons?

Let's suppose you graduated from "The Paulette La France Beauty Academy" to become a hair stylist. Would you need to schedule monthly hair-styling lessons with Paulette? If you received the proper training, why would you continue to need Paulette?

If your instructors have not rendered themselves unnecessary after a certain time, something's amiss in what you're learning and how you're learning it. Viable teaching and learning models obviate continuous instruction. To improve, you must actualize deep learning.

I'm not suggesting that learning to play golf is comparable to learning kite flying or hair styling. I'm suggesting that you need to revisit your thinking and learning habits. To acquire complex skills, merge discovery and mastery. Discovery is cognitive. Mastery is kinesthetic.

Reportedly, Bobby Jones mastered the golf swing by swinging a rope. Since a flexible rope can't be leveraged—like a rigid pry bar—you must swing it. Ben Hogan likened the motion of his trailing arm in the downswing to skipping a stone. Create new engrams or memory traces by adopting familiar and analogous movements to master the swing's subconscious sensations and muscle sequences. To achieve mastery, experiment with sticky and analogous transfer skills.

Your *experiencing-self* is your *remembering-self*. Rely more on feelings and mental images and less on words and thoughts. Hidden within most stymied golfers—who use conscious controls, self-talk, and mechanical movements—there's a relaxed golfer using subconscious controls, sticky visualizations, and automatic movements waiting to break out.

Since you inherently know that holding conscious and multiple swing thoughts in your brain doesn't work, refine your learning to support your instincts. Golfers who rely exclusively on conscious cues are prisoners of their beliefs. If you're stagnating, try something new.

Bill Mehlhorn, a legendary golfer in the 1920s and 1930s, claimed that the grass whip is the optimum swing-trainer. Recently, Bobby Shave, a PGA professional, former college golf coach, and Mehlhorn protégé, has preserved Mehlhorn's legacy.

Many instructors suggest that swinging a grass whip may be the easiest and best to way to *experience* the sensations associated with a holisitic golf swing.

A grass whip is a simple garden tool consisting of a wooden handle, steel shaft, and double-sided serrated flat blade designed to cut grass in a back-and-forth motion. Used as a golf training aid, it imparts the sensations, movements, positions, and forces associated with a repeatable and effective golf swing. When you swing a grass whip, you're performing a variation of the "L to L Drill."

Pretend the grass whip is a club by stepping forward and swinging it from side to side to cut grass. You'll experience the proper hip rotation, wrist and hand action, forearm rotation, shoulder turn, posture, tempo, and timing. Focus only on cutting grass in both directions. If you're not cutting grass in both directions, you're doing it incorrectly.

When you employ a grass whip, focus on how your heels lift and knees bend as you walk. In a natural walking motion, the first thing that moves is your lead heel. To start your swing, simply lift up your lead heel. Great players lift their heels. Poor players plant their heels.

Swinging a grass whip will impart rapid learning. First, you'll learn to set your feet apart at shoulder width to enhance your mobility. Second, you'll learn to stand relatively erect and bend at the waist. Third, you'll learn to lift up your heels, swivel your ankles, bend your knees, and shift your weight from side to side as if you were riding a bike. Fourth, you'll learn to swing along a curved path. Fifth, you'll learn to use your ankles, knees, and hips to move your chest and in turn move your arms. Sixth, you'll learn to move your navel. Seventh, you'll learn how to use your hands.

Most important, use a grass whip to learn the release, the most misunderstood aspect of the golf swing. The release is a *tumbling*—not a *flipping*—motion. Make your trailing hand climb over your lead hand. A tumbling motion inverts or rotates the entire golf club 180 degrees, thereby employing it as a powerful *four-foot* lever. A flipping motion rotates only the clubhead 180 degrees, thereby employing it as a weak *four-inch* lever.

To understand the release, imagine that you're using a four-foot dowel to sweep a row of upright soda cans off a work-bench. To knock them over, imagine using only your hands to rotate the entire dowel from end to end or 180 degrees. To release the dowel with power, you must roll your lead wrist axle, whip your lead elbow, and supinate your lead forearm.

The key difference in the analogy between the dowel and the golf club is the orientation of the shaft. To release the dowel—positioned at a 90-degree angle to the workbench—you must swing on a level plane. To release a golf club—positioned at a 45-degree angle to the ground—you must swing downward on an angular plane. In releasing both dowel and club, however, everything else is essentially the same.

Since you can't flip the serrated blade of a grass whip, you'll learn to scroll the shaft. When you use a grass whip, step for-ward, shift your weight back and forth naturally, and pump your knees forward and backward.

The legendary Mike Austin likened the weight shift, knee action, and footwork in the golf swing to that of pedal-ing a bike. Pumping his powerful legs in a pedaling motion, Austin would rotate his trailing knee and thigh into the ball. Harnessing the pumping action of his legs, Austin at age 64 hit the longest recorded drive of 515 yards during a PGA event. Hogan used the term "coming at the ball" to denote driving his trailing knee directly into the ball at impact.

Swinging a grass whip will teach you how to lift up your heels, shift your weight, remain balanced, use the joints and levers of your lower body, and turn your navel.

Using a grass whip will generate new brain cells and neu-ral pathways as you consolidate many different movement patterns, namely, *remaining* in balance, *steadying* your head, *turning* your torso, *swinging* your arms, *educating* your hands, *pumping* your legs, *lifting* your heels, *harnessing* your lower body, *shifting* your weight, and *executing* your follow-through. Merging these disparate movements over time will boost neurogenesis.

The grass whip may be the missing piece to learning, unlearning, and relearning the golf swing. Bobby Shave and Wild Bill Mehlhorn—leading exponents of the grass whip as a training aid—may be the most important, yet least-known, mentors in your golfing renaissance.

Smarts

My golfing friend, a brilliant neurologist, earned his under-graduate degree from Harvard, received a medical degree from Dartmouth, served a one-year internship at Yale New Haven Hospital, and spent three years at NYU's Langone Medical Center researching stroke, epilepsy, and movement disorders.

Ironically, my intelligent and well-educated friend has an atrocious golf swing. It makes Charles Barkley's snake-coil, death-spiral, rump-twirl look good. Unfortunately, my friend is unable and unwilling to recognize and fix his glaring swing problems. How can such a brilliant individual be so clueless? Golf invariably exposes your true personality. If you don't want your character to show, don't play golf.

Albert Einstein said, "Two things are infinite: the universe and human stupidity. And I'm not sure about the universe."

Psychologists have theorized why smart people make dumb mistakes. Travis Bradberry, in his article "Why Smart People Act So Stupid" posted on BBC Capitol, said, "It's good to be smart. After all, intelligent people earn more money, accumu-late more wealth, and even live longer. But there's another side to the story. Intelligent people have a reputation for making dumb mistakes, especially in situations that require common sense."

Researchers confirm that rational thinking and intelligence do not go hand in hand. Two university studies regarding the problem-solving behaviors of various individuals found that smart people grossly overrate their intellectual abilities. Consequently, they're more inclined to blurt out poorly reasoned and incorrect solutions. Extremely smart people, long accustomed to knowing the right answers and receiving praise for their smarts, often develop inflated views of their talents. Many smart people are ignorant prima donnas.

If brilliant people can't recognize and fix their swing flaws, who can? Often smart people have difficulty admitting their flaws and accepting help. Know-it-all golfers tend to eschew feedback and lack self-awareness. Highly intelligent golfers tend to overlook their ignorance.

Highly intelligent people who are high achievers and well-paid professionals revel in their success. Consequently, they underestimate the inherent difficulty associated with learning swing mechanics. Since they've learned everything analytically, they wrongly assume they can learn swing mechanics analytically. Learning the golf swing requires analytical and systemic thinking.

In his book *What Intelligence Tests Miss: The Psychology of Rational Thought* (2009), Keith Stanovich argues that IQ tests do not measure one's rational thinking skills and cognitive ability. For example, "The Unabomber," Theodore Kaczynski, had an IQ of 161. But his impressive IQ did not make him a rational thinker. There's an enormous difference between intelligence and rationality.

Stanovich coined the term "dysrationalia" to denote one's inability to think and behave rationally despite having adequate intelligence. Don't assume that your superior

IQ and lofty academic credentials will make you an expert golfer.

Consider the case of my friend Artie Bono, reigning club champion for the last four years. Artie is the antithesis of my neurologist golfing friend. Artie's high school academic record and SAT scores were so low that Moosick County Community College, which has an open admission policy, rejected him.

The Transition

Your mother-in-law just called from Bolduc's Transmission. She needs a ride. Apparently, she slammed her shift lever into reverse at fast idle when she was trying to snag a parking spot at *The Furry Fiesta* (where she buys organic cat food). The last time she wrecked her transmission, it cost her $3,600 for a replacement, mountings, driveline components, gear sets, and labor. Your golf swing may also have a serious transmission problem.

Newton's Laws of Motion dictate that when a moving object reverses direction, it must first decelerate and momentarily pause. Unfortunately, your mother-in-law doesn't understand that.

Therefore, the split-second transfer of power and change of direction at the top of your swing must be slow, steady, and smooth—not rapid, impulsive, and violent. When you transition between your backswing and downswing, you must shift gears smoothly.

Physicists often compare the swinging motion of a golf club to that of a pendulum (i.e., an object suspended from a fixed point that swings back and forth). A golf club and a pendulum are both affected by gravity and momentum.

Generally speaking, the golf swing employs a two-pendulum system. Your *upper* pendulum—attached at a fixed pivot point near your sternum—is an isosceles triangle formed by your arms and shoulder girdle. Your *lower* pendulum is the club clasped at the hands and hinged loosely by the wrists. When your upper pendulum momentarily slows up in the downswing, it generates centrifugal force that accelerates your lower pendulum.

"Let the pendulum swing" was Mike Austin's famous mantra. Austin urged his pupils to execute the transition by employing an underhanded throwing motion. As your body turns, throw the clubhead underhanded along a circular path with your right hand as you extend your arms and unfold your elbows.

Centrifugal force, emanating from your body, transmits a wave of energy through the shaft, into the clubhead, and to the ball. To swing effectively, you must synchronize both pendulums. Be advised that most synchronization problems occur during the transition.

The secret to proper synchronization is tempo. Most golfers routinely ignore the critical dimension of *time* in their swing. Every elegant swing is suffused with the exquisite element of time.

When you exhibit Neanderthal impulses, you'll speed up your backswing, rush your transition, and force the club. Brute and atavistic hit impulses create problems.

If Vinnie hitting range balls and a caveman bludgeoning a mastodon were standing side by side, their swings would look identical. A caveman, driven by self-preservation, can ignore tempo and transition. Cavemen employed rapid, powerful, and savage muscle-movement patterns.

However, golfers can't. You're not swinging a war club. You're letting a pendulum swing. To swing your club like a pendulum, your muscle-movement patterns must be slow and steady. Physicists use the term *resonance* to denote a pendulum's natural rhythm.

In a *make-it-happen* mode, you employ *force* to execute your backswing. Consequently, your transition is abrupt and jerky. In a *let-it-happen* mode, you employ *inertia* and *momentum* to execute the backswing and achieve a relaxed and smooth transition. To experience "flow," the sublime merging of mind and body, you need exquisite tempo.

In their book *Tour Tempo: Golf's Last Secret Finally Revealed* (2003), John Novosel and John Garrity share their research about the tempos of Tour pros. They assert that Tour pros have a 3-to-1 backswing-to-downswing tempo. In other words, their backswings take three times longer than their downswings. Whether you swing rapidly like Nick Price or slowly like Ernie Els, you still need a 3-to-1 ratio.

Yale University researchers Robert D. Grober and Jacek Cholewicki confirmed the findings from *Tour Tempo* in their article titled "Towards a Biomechanical Understanding of Tempo in the Golf Swing." Grober and Cholewicki determined that the ideal backswing should last approximately .75 seconds and the ideal downswing should last approximately .25 seconds. These findings confirm Novosel's 3-to-1 ratio. Tour pros, whose swings last between 1.0 and 1.4 seconds, devote 30 percent of their time to their transition.

Grober and Cholewicki write, ". . . the tempo of the golf swing of professional golfers exhibits remarkable uniformity in 1) the absolute time scale, 2) the ratio of backswing time to downswing time, and 3) the invariance of these times as a function of the length of the swing. These observations suggest that professional golfers have at the core of their golf swing a biomechanical clock."

An abrupt transition, whether you're using large or small muscles, destroys your tempo. You must pause momentarily in your transition. You need a static position at the top to change direction and use ground forces. No pause = No ground forces.

To develop a smooth transition, you must generate new brain cells and introduce new neural firing patterns. You can't erase the existing memory traces associated with your fast and abrupt transition. Therefore, you must create new memory traces, new synaptic connections, and new firing patterns. Changing your tempo requires willpower, focus, and patience.

To master the transition—to induce the requisite neurogenesis—consider buying an inexpensive, pocket-sized metronome to actualize auditory learning. You can buy a Korg MA-1 metronome online for under $25. If your transition is slow and smooth, you can swing as hard as you want in your downswing. *In your transition, ensure that your trailing elbow stays UNDER your lead elbow.*

Heading home from Bolduch's Transmission, your mother-in-law, who has a $5 coupon for organic cat food in her purse, will undoubtedly make you stop at The Furry Fiesta. Spooky gets only the best.

Practice

Two days before "The Frank Zumbo Two-Ball," Mario booked a lesson with the head pro. His $75 session, reportedly the best money he ever spent, produced magical results on the range. Unfortunately, things didn't pan out on the course.

In his opening round, Mario had one *Amelia Earhart* (a drive that looks good taking off, then disappears), four *Danny Devitos* (nasty five-footers), and six *Pump Handles* (sevens). Mario claimed he needed more *swing oil* (i.e., Bud Lite) before he teed off.

On the practice range you hit balls; on the course, you play shots is an adage that applies to most golfers. The inability to transfer your skills from the range to the course suggests you're employing flawed techniques.

In 1993, Dr. K. Anders Ericsson, a research psychologist and performance expert at Florida State University, published "The Role of Deliberate Practice in the Acquisition Expert Performance." Ericsson maintains that you need 10,000 hours and/or ten years of deliberate practice to achieve world-class expertise. That's 90 minutes a day for twenty years!

In *Outliers* (2008), Malcolm Gladwell promulgated *The 10,000-Hour Rule* based on Ericsson's research. Gladwell states that 10,000 hours is "the magic number for greatness."

He examines how extraordinary people or outliers achieve proficiency in certain subjects and skills by devoting 10,000 hours to practicing. Gladwell claims that 10,000 hours represents the "tipping point" of greatness.

Ericsson criticized Gladwell's "10,000-Hour Rule" in the following rebuke: "A popularized but simplistic view of our work, which suggests that anyone who has accumulated a sufficient number of hours of practice in a given domain will automatically become an expert and a champion."

Ericsson accused Gladwell of distorting his research findings. According to Ericsson, 10,000 hours was the *average*—not the actual number—of practice hours that experts invested to achieve mastery. Some experts practiced fewer hours; others practiced for over 25,000 hours. Most important, Ericsson faults Gladwell for failing to distinguish between the quantity and quality of practice time. You may need 10,000 hours to qualify for the US Open—but not to achieve competency.

To learn a new motor skill, you must change your brain's deep wiring system. When you first learn a motor skill, your movements are stiff and awkward. With considerable practice, your movements become smooth and flowing. Practice helps the brain optimize motor movements through a process called *myelination*.

Your brain has billions of building blocks or neurons containing thousands of dendrites that receive signals from other neurons. Axons are long neural fibers that connect with the dendrites of other neurons. Neurons coordinate, communicate, and connect by sending electrical impulses through axons. When neurons fire, they resemble closely stacked, rapidly falling dominoes.

The outside of your brain, comprised of neurons, looks gray. The inside of your brain, comprised of myelin, is white. Myelin is the fatty tissue-like wiring insulation that covers the lengthy strands of axons. Myelination, namely, the thickening of your axons' outer layers, increases the speed and strength of the nerve impulses that jump across neurons. As neurons connect in greater frequency, myelin layers thicken.

How does all this relate to practice? With increased practice, two things happen: (1) neural impulses multiply and speed up and (2) myelin layers build up around axons.

Jason Shen, a neuroscientist, claims that MRI studies performed on the brains of musicians reveal a clear connection between practice and performance. "Most significantly, there was a direct correlation between how many hours they [expert pianists] practiced and how dense their white/myelin matter was."

Understand, however, that myelination depends on the *quantity* and *quality* of your practice. Unless you process practical feedback during focused and motivated practice sessions, myelination will not occur.

There are two distinct forms of practice. *Deliberate* practice is monitored, productive, slow, purposeful, systematic, and focused. *Regular* practice is unmonitored, unproductive, rapid, robotic, random, and unfocused. Let's briefly examine what golf experts and neuroscientists say about practice.

Butch Harmon advises golfers to attend PGA events to observe the deliberate practice routines of Tour pros. When Tour pros practice, they hit only 25 to 30 shots per hour and pause between shots. When expert golfers practice their irons, for example, they work on hitting the ball first, staying in balance, and maintaining a smooth tempo.

To maximize your practice time and effort, most instructors suggest working first on your short game. This approach, however, is antithetical to most golfers who consider putting and chipping boring. Golfers prefer to swing their driver—their Ball Masher, Bazooka Joe, Thunder Stick, Grenade Launcher, Fat Boy, Frick Hammer, Whopper Popper, Calf Killer, Blaster Master, Goat Humper, or Zeus Wang.

In his *NYT* article "At the Range, Drive Less and Practice More," Bill Pennington quotes PGA instructor Mike Bender: "Here's what people have to understand: the full swing is 80 percent technique and 20 percent feel, and the short game is 80 percent feel and 20 percent technique. Improving your short-game feel is much easier and will make your scores drop right away. On the range, people often aren't sure what's going on. Even a bad swing produces good results a few times. Then people try to recapture that moment for the next hour or more. They're spinning their wheels."

Unrealistic, unproductive, and autopilot practice (i.e., hitting the same club over and over) imparts a false sense of confidence. Therefore, you must periodically switch clubs to simulate actual play. Golfers who repeatedly hit the same club are like pianists who repeatedly practice "Mary Had a Little Lamb." What's the point?

Most important, deliberate practice implies self-discovery, critical observation, cause-and-effect reasoning, experimentation, testing, and note taking. Practice smarter and better—not faster, longer, and harder.

Next, let's consider the recent findings of research scientists on making practice more efficient. Dr. Pablo Celnik, a Johns Hopkins University medical school professor, recently conducted an experiment assessing the practice skills of 86 subjects. Celnik found that people who master complex skills most effectively make *slight changes* in their practice routines rather than adhere to the same routine.

In *Current Biology*, Celnik writes, "What we found is [that] if you practice a *slightly modified version* of a task you want to master, you actually learn more and faster than if you just keep practicing the exact same thing multiple times in a row." Celnik's findings have key implications not only for golfers learning complex skills sets, but also for stroke patients learning new motor functions.

In his study, Celnik asked 86 volunteers to learn a computer-based motor skill associated with moving a cursor. He randomly divided his subjects into two groups. *Group One*, having received their initial training instructions, practiced for six hours. *Group Two*, having received their initial training instructions, subsequently received slightly different instructions.

Celnik discovered that *Group Two* participants, who had to adjust their practice session, performed their tasks with greater accuracy than and at twice the speed of those in the other groups. Based on his experiment, Celnik postulated his "Theory of Reconsolidation" whereby existing memories are recalled and modified with new knowledge.

When you practice the same routine, you *consolidate* memories. Conversely, when you introduce new knowledge and make subtle changes in your practice routine, you *reconsolidate* memories. "Our results are important because little was known before about how re-consolidation works in relation to motor skill development. This shows how simple manipulations during training can lead to more rapid and larger motor skill gains because of reconsolidation," says Celnik.

Nicholas Wymbs and Amy Bastian, in "Want to Learn a New Skill? Faster? Change Up Your Practice Sessions" (*Johns Hopkins News Release*), write, "Alterations in training have to be small, something akin to slightly adjusting the size or weight of a baseball bat, tennis racket, or soccer ball in between practice sessions." Current studies by Celnik's team suggest that drastically changing practice sessions, such as playing badminton in between tennis matches or playing badminton with a tennis racket, brings no significant benefit to motor learning.

Celnik writes, "What we found is if you practice a slightly modified version of a task you want to master, you actually learn more and faster than if you just keep practicing the exact same thing multiple times in a row." Introducing variations in your practice routine—putting, chipping, pitching, and driving—will nearly *double* the speed at which you learn.

In his article "Practice, Made Perfect?" (*Time*, 2013), Sean Gregory discusses this variable mode of practice called *interleaving* that involves mixing things up. Researchers studied the performance of college baseball players who took *blocked* and *interleaving* batting practice. In *blocked* practice, hitters faced 45 pitches: 15 fastballs, then 15 curveballs, then 15 change-ups. In *interleaving* practice, hitters faced 45 random pitches. The players who took interleaving batting practice performed much better in game situations.

When you *interleave* multiple and related skills, you learn faster and better. Gregory writes, "Interleaving gives the brain a better workout because mixing tasks provides just enough stress to trigger the release of a hormone called corticotropin releasing factor (CRF) in the hippocampus, the brain area central to memory and learning. CRF strengthens synapses."

During blocked practice, by contrast, you're not reloading your circuitry by trying different tasks, you're under less stress, and your brain is bored and less engaged.

Educational psychologist Dr. Doug Rohrer asserts that students preparing for exams in multiple subjects (e.g., math, history, physics, and English) earned higher scores by studying a bit of each subject each day rather than studying a single subject for an entire day. *The key to successful practice is variation, not repetition.*

University of Pittsburgh Medical School researchers claim that practice not only makes perfect, but also increases neuronal activity in the motor cortex that plans and executes movements. In other words, when you practice visually guided motor tasks, your "plastic" motor cortex stores repetitive movement patterns.

The more you practice selected movements, the fewer neural input signals your primary motor cortex requires. Dr. Strick states, ". . . our results indicate that practice changes the primary motor cortex so that it can become an important substrate of motor skills. Thus, the motor cortex is adaptable or plastic." In sum, practice makes the motor cortex more efficient.

To enhance your skill sets, employ the *deliberate* practice techniques espoused by Tour pros and the *reconsolidation* practice techniques espoused by neuroscientists.

A recent study, conducted by Dr. Brooke McNamara, Dr. David Hambrick, and Dr. Frederick Oswald, found that deliberate practice might be overrated in building expertise. In "Becoming an Expert Takes More Than Practice" (*Psychological Science*), they assert that the number of deliberate practice hours is important, but not as important as many suppose.

Seeking to discover patterns among a range of experts, McNamara and her team analyzed 88 scientific studies that examined practice routines in music, games, sports, education, and other areas. Having completed their "megastudy," they determined that the more people practice, depending on their specific domain, the more they improved.

For example, they found that practice accounts for about 26 percent of individual differences among expert performers in the area of games, 21 percent in the area of music, 18 percent in the area of sport, 4 percent in the area of education, and only 1 percent in the professional area. Overall, practice accounts for only 12 percent of individual differences among expert performers across a wide range of domains.

McNamara and her colleagues conclude that many factors associated with practice (e.g., quantity, quality, domain, memory, age, genetics, and cognitive ability) drive improvement.

In a nutshell, the brain's motor cortex becomes more efficient and movement patterns more automatic with practice. Therefore, it's imperative that you practice only correct movements. Incorrect and deeply rooted movement patterns are difficult to overwrite.

Eye Tracking

When Fat Tony, your 415-pound golfing buddy, danced at Bobby Fusco's wedding, you couldn't believe your eyes. During the reception, Fat Tony danced The Chicken Walk, The Car Wash, The Hokey Pokey, The Monkey, The Limbo, The Moon Walk, The Electric Slide, The Watusi, The Achy Breaky Heart, The Loco-Motion, and The Hully Gully. Unfortunately, the band quit before Tony could do the Michael Jackson Thriller dance.

Too cheap to take lessons, Fat Tony learned to dance by watching "Dancing with the Stars" and focusing on foot movements. By fixating on how dancers moved their feet, Fat Tony quickly learned twenty different dances. Recent eye-tracking studies confirm Fat Tony's claim that *gaze patterns* optimize the acquisition of complex motor skills.

Eye tracking, a key component of observational learning, denotes the process of assessing and measuring gazing patterns. Researchers contend that many expert athletes learn complex motor skills by employing efficient gaze patterns that target relevant muscle movements. Nick Faldo claims, "In golf, our eyes are probably our most important asset."

In their seminal study, "Looking to Learn: The Effects of Visual Guidance on Observational Learning of the Golf Swing," UK researchers Giorgia D'Innocenzo, Claudia C. Gonzalez,

Mark Williams, and Daniel T. Bishop, using pretest and post-test protocols, compared two sets of golfers: (1) golfers viewing swing videos with superimposed, color-coded eye-tracking cues and (2) golfers viewing videos without colored-coded visual cues.

These researchers determined that golfers viewing videos with directed-gaze, color-coded cues experienced superior learning. Simply put, golf videos containing color-coded and highlighted areas that direct your focus provide enhanced learning.

The authors write, "In observational learning contexts, such ineffective gaze behavior may prevent or inhibit the acquisition of relevant information. Therefore, by directing the learner's visual attention to task-relevant regions, observational learning of motor skills may be improved. Accordingly, our aim was to determine whether exogenous guidance may be used to train gaze behavior during a video modeling intervention, and whether this, in turn, would facilitate novices' observational learning the golf swing."

When you watch golf videos, hone your visual acuities. Employ *directed gazing* at specific and relevant areas—not *scattered gazing* at generalized and irrelevant areas.

The UK team writes, "Researchers have shown that elite performers tend to exhibit more effective gaze patterns than their novice counterparts. Specifically, when trying to anticipate an opponent's next action, someone who is perceptually skilled often requires fewer fixations of longer duration in order to extract task-relevant information, which indicates an underlying efficiency to their gaze behavior. Moreover, when compared to less-skilled performers, experts are more adept at ignoring redundant/task-irrelevant stimuli."

To gain the optimal fixation points for selected swing movements, view mostly edited videos using color-coded cues and eschew the rest. To enhance your observational learning, *retrain* your gazing patterns and activate your anatomical zoom lens.

Dr. Joan Vickers, a pioneering cognitive scientist at the University of Calgary, developed the concept known as the quiet-eye theory. Using eye-tracking technology, Vickers found that fixating on relevant visual stimuli at the right time—usually a few hundred milliseconds before, during, and after executing a complex motor movement—improves an athlete's chances of success.

Vickers says, "When your eyes provide the data, your motor system just knows what to do. Your brain is like a GPS system. It detects target, speed, intensity, and distance."

To enhance your observational learning indoors, employ a laser pointer mounted inside a training grip. At a pet store, buy a cat-toy laser to insert into your training grip. Pointing the laser *downward* will help you visualize the swing path of the clubhead. Pointing the laser *inward* or at your navel will help you visualize the swing path of the end-cap. Practice in slow motion and at regular speed to vividly imprint the mental images of the swing paths for the clubhead and end-cap.

Pointed Downward. In your *setup*, point the laser at the ball. In your *backswing*, trace the target line with the laser. With your right palm adjacent to your right shoulder facing the target line at the top, start your *downswing* by pointing the laser at the target line. The laser pointer will descend the swing arc on a 45-degree angle. When you reach the *delivery* position—with your right palm facing skyward—point the laser at the target line. In your *follow-through*—when your right palm crosses over your left—continue to trace the target line with the laser. In your *finish*, point the laser over your front shoulder.

Pointed Inward. In your *setup*, point the laser at your navel. In your *backswing*, trace the target line with the laser. In your *downswing*—as your hands transit between your rear foot and front foot—point the laser at your navel. (The inward laser must never point beyond the midline of your chest.) In your *follow-through*—when your palms rapidly cross over and the shaft reverses—point the laser away from your navel to trace the target line.

The quiet-eye concept, however, encompasses not only vision, but also attention. Fixating your gaze enhances the brain's ability to concentrate on essential details and eliminate distractions. Dr. Mark Wilson, a psychology professor at the University of Exeter, suggests that quiet-eye techniques stimulate the dorsal area of the brain associated with goal-directed attention and physiological functions such as heart rate and muscle movements.

Quiet-eye skills—albeit somewhat difficult to master—are teachable. Wilson claims that that quiet-eye exercises may improve one's performance in basketball shooting, golf, marksmanship, and surgery. Wilson has trained professional golfers, Olympic athletes, and soldiers in quiet-eye techniques.

Quiet eye also helps athletes perform better under pressure. Scientists claim that athletes choke because pressure degrades attention. Recent studies indicate that even novice golfers can rapidly improve their scores by learning how to use their eyes in putting. In 2014, when Ernie Els was struggling, he was not on anyone's short list to win the U.S. Open. During his acceptance speech, Els attributed his win to "eye exercises" he'd been working on with visual skills coach Dr. Sherylle Calder.

Els, who now employs Calder full-time, uses eye exercises to sharpen his putting regimen. Calder's visual training program includes software that works on his reaction times and visual sharpness. In one exercise, Calder projects different sports balls and shapes on a computer screen and asks Els to hit them with the cursor and recall a number that appears shortly after.

A sample of golfers who used Joan Vickers's quiet-eye technique to improve their putting sank 16 percent more putts and reduced their average number of putts by 3 per round. Vickers found that elite golfers have a more intense gaze on the ball and its path to the cup.

Vickers advises golfers to (1) focus briefly on the *exact* spot where they wish to send the ball, (2) settle their eyes again on the ball, and (3) hold their eyes there. Intense focus on the ball blocks out negative interference from mental chatter and "allows the brain to process the aiming information and direct the body in the proper motions to get the ball where you wish to go."

Dr. Mark Wilson, another movement scientist, conducted a quiet-eye study using two groups of golfers. Group One practiced different aspects of their putting stroke. Group Two, who ignored their putting stroke, practiced visualization techniques. The results were convincing. Golfers who focused on visualization techniques were more accurate than those who focused on their stroke. According to Wilson, golfers who employ quiet-eye techniques have lower heart rates, less muscle twitching, and less performance anxiety. Better golfers putt by keeping their eyes focused longer on the back of the ball.

Dr. Wilson encourages golfers to keep their gaze on the exact contact point on the back of the ball for a brief period or just enough time to say to themselves, "the back of the cup," before they start their stroke. Immediately after each putt and before golfers know where the ball goes, Wilson advises golfers to grade themselves on the quality of their strike based on a 1–10 scale. Make the quality of your stroke—not whether you sink the putt—your main putting goal.

Imitate the world's best putters by (1) rapidly alternating your gaze between the back of the ball and the target, (2) fixating on the ball for 2 to 3 seconds, then (3) holding your position for another 1 to 2 seconds after stroking the putt. To putt effectively, quiet not only your eyes, but also your mind.

Accordingly, don't keep your eye *and* mind on the ball. To avoid becoming ball-bound, keep your eye on the ball and your mind on the target.

Sherlock Holmes

Bobby "Sherlock" Bovenzi is a licensed commercial bedbug inspector. (He also inspects for lice, but bedbugs are his specialty.) He earned his nickname "Sherlock" not for his ability to exterminate elusive bedbugs, but for his uncanny ability to spot and remediate golf swing problems.

For example, when Sherlock observed the groove marks on Vito's sand wedge, he realized Vito's angle of approach was too steep. When he observed the outer spike on Rusty's right golf shoe, he knew Rusty wasn't pivoting properly. When he observed a bottle of Valium in Mario's golf bag, he knew Mario's mother-in-law was in town.

To improve your game, sharpen your powers of *observation* and *deduction*. Sherlock Holmes, Sir Arthur Conan Doyle's mastermind detective, is an ideal cognitive model for stymied golfers. I'm not suggesting that you adopt the quirky and obsessive habits of Sherlock Holmes. Rather, I'm suggesting you learn to observe and deduce more critically. To solve your golf problems, become a detective.

When I recently saw a set of irons previously owned by Tiger Woods on eBay, I noticed something interesting. The wear marks on Tiger's irons, unlike those on mine, were tightly concentrated in an area *low* on the clubface.

Upon further investigation, I deduced that expert golfers strike the ball *low* on the clubface because they hit the ball before they take a divot. Expert golfers close the face and hit down on the ball. However, the marks on the clubs of most amateurs usually contain (1) scratches from hitting rocks in the rough, (2) high wear marks on the face, and (3) various sweet spots from inconsistent contact.

In her book *Mastermind: How to Think Like Sherlock Holmes* (2013), psychologist Maria Konnikova contrasts the mindsets of Dr. Watson and Sherlock Holmes. Watson—gullible, impulsive, and obtuse—exhibits superficial thinking by openly accepting most of what he sees and hears. Sherlock Holmes—skeptical, methodical, and inquisitive—exhibits deep thinking by questioning most of what he sees and hears.

"Holmes's trick is to treat every thought, every experience, and every perception," Konnikova states, "the way he would [view] a pink elephant. In other words, begin with a healthy dose of skepticism instead of the credulity that is your mind's natural state of being."

Before you change your swing methodology, practice routine, or equipment, exercise skepticism, discernment, and patience. Use a Sherlock Holmes Mindset. Einstein wrote, "The important thing is to not stop questioning. Curiosity has its own reason for existing."

In "A Study in Scarlet," Holmes compares the mind of an *inferior* thinker to an attic cluttered with useless junk. Conversely, he compares the mind of a *superior* thinker to an orderly attic containing useful tools and important keepsakes. In your mental attic, store relevant and useful principles, habits, and techniques—then discard the rest.

Holmes, according to Konnikova, exhibits many concepts that psychologists have only recently discovered, such as "correspondence bias"—using your behavior to interpret that of others—and "omission neglect"—ignoring key information.

For example, when Watson blindly accepts the testimony of an attractive female witness, Holmes cautions Watson about being swayed by her comely appearance. When Holmes famously questions why a dog in the presence of an intruder didn't bark, he discovers a major piece of evidence.

In her article "8 Strategies for Thinking More Like Sherlock Holmes," psychologist Susan Perry offers stymied golfers the following relevant advice: remain skeptical, recognize biases, draw logical conclusions, employ sensory feedback, avoid distractions, broaden your perspective, refresh stale thinking, and take notes.

To imitate Sherlock Holmes, remain inquisitive. "I have no special talents," Einstein once told a friend in a letter. "I'm just passionately curious." Ben Hogan, whose signature talent was inquisitiveness, had a genius-level IQ.

According to neuroscientists, when your brain experiences a buzz of curiosity, your dopamine receptors react as if you were eating a chocolate bar.

Pretend you're a golf detective by asking yourself what your golf glove, callouses, grips, golf shoes, clubface marks, divots, ball flight patterns, and missed putts are telling you about your game. Adopt a Sherlock Holmes mindset to discover what's happening right under your nose.

Adroit golfers have the ability to understand *causality*. Causal reasoning—the process of identifying cause-and-effect relationships—links ancient philosophy and modern neuroscience. To improve your game, pretend you're Sherlock Holmes by making logical inferences and deductions.

If Bobby "Sherlock" Bovenzi, a licensed, certified bedbug inspector with uncanny observational and deductive powers, can diagnose swing flaws, you can, too.

Arcs and Straight Lines

Dogmatic beliefs are unsupported and accepted opinions masquerading as ultimate truths. When you hold dogmatic truths, you close your mind to alternative perspectives and fresh ideas.

Consider these irrational dogmatic statements: *There are no secrets to success. There are no honest politicians. There are no guarantees in life. There are no free lunches. There are no insoluble problems. There are no perfect marriages. There are no easy roads in life.*

In golf, there are two key dogmatic beliefs: *There are no straight lines in the golf swing* and *Straight lines produce curved shots, and curved lines produce straight shots.*

You need to test dogmatic beliefs for yourself. If you blindly accept these dogmatic beliefs or half-truths, you'll mistakenly purge all straight lines—including the target line, toe line, eye line, shaft plane line, elbow plane line, shoulder line, putting line, line of flight, ball-marker lines, and lead shoulder-to-ball line at impact—from your consciousness.

You need *relatively* straight lines to flatten your lead wrist, straighten your elbows, extend your arms, release lag, straighten your legs, create a flat spot for your driver, and finish in a standing position. In your 3-D swing, it's easier for your brain to visualize straight lines and angles than curved lines or arcs.

At address, form a relatively straight line extending from your lead shoulder (i.e., glenohumeral joint) to the clubhead. At impact—with your hands raised slightly and pushed forward, with your lead wrist bowed, and with the shaft leaning forward—restore the straight line extending from your lead shoulder to the clubhead. This is your "radius of power."

To establish a fixed radius within your swing path, employ a "shoulder pinch" or "pec grab" at address by connecting the socket of your lead shoulder to your chest wall. Your *upper lead arm*—connected to your chest wall—will remain relatively straight; however, it will soften and bend at the elbow during the swing. Your forearms—which are bent at the elbows to form your swing triangle—are often called "alligator arms."

Babe Ruth advised Sam Byrd, his New York Yankees teammate, to tuck a towel under his left armpit. Sam Byrd, using precisely what Babe Ruth taught him, became a highly successful PGA professional who won 25 tour events. Byrd later told noted sportswriter Grantland Rice, *"I tuck a towel under my left armpit, square up my right foot, shift my body into the brace right leg for power and my left arm stays on my body the whole time while hinging at the elbow—and I go to the target."* Practice this!

To ascribe a circular swing, brush your lead arm against your chest and keep your lead arm under your lead hand. Swing your lead shoulder along a tight in-curve. Your clubhead forms the circumference of your swing. However, you need a fixed radius to inscribe a circle.

Imagine drawing a circle with a geometric compass. The needle arm establishes the radius as the pencil arm traces the circumference. The needle and pencil arms are tangible and obvious. What isn't intangible and obvious is the *radius* or distance between the points of the needle and the tip of the pencil. In the golf swing, your lead arm and club shaft—which inscribe the circumference—are tangible and obvious. The hidden part of your swing circle is the invisible line—or fixed radius—between your Adam's apple and lead wrist.

Swinging your arms independently and separating them from your torso will distort your swing radius. To keep the club on plane, maintain a fixed radius by preserving a straight line between your lead wrist and your Adam's apple.

Moe Norman became a great ball-striker by envisioning a flat spot at the bottom of his swing. Norman kept his clubface square to the target line for approximately 23 inches before and after impact. Norman referred to this flat spot as "the business end of the golf swing." To improve your ball-striking, embed a flat spot—or straight line—at the bottom of your elliptical swing. You can't build an accurate house or swing without an accurate blueprint.

Form another straight line at impact. To create a forward-leaning straight line at impact, you need a firm lead side, flat lead wrist, slightly bent trailing elbow, and modest hip turn. To create this straight line, return your lead shoulder at impact to its original address position. At impact, ensure that your trailing thumb forms a straight line with the radius bone of your trailing elbow and your lead thumb forms a straight line with the radius bone of your lead forearm.

Postimpact, when the clubhead is farthest away from your sternum, extend both arms and rehinge your wrists into the follow-through. To release literally means to *let go*. In your release, you're letting go of lag. However, the release denotes far more than just letting go. It denotes *straightening* your elbows and *extending* both arms several feet beyond impact.

If you were using a broomstick to smack a dusty rug hanging on a clothesline, what would you do? To transfer the energy from your body to the broomstick and into the rug, you would stabilize your lead shoulder, straighten your elbows, flatten your lead wrist, rotate your wrist axles, and extend both arms.

Deciding between arcs and straight lines is like deciding whether your dog is comprised of curves or straight lines. Dualistic or "either-or" thinking—the most basic form of reasoning—narrows your options and solutions. Integrative thinking merges alternatives and expands your options and solutions. Now let's examine the arcs and curves in the swing.

Physicists assert that the swing path is actually elliptical. If your swing path were circular, which it's not, it would have a *constant* radius. Your elliptical swing path has a *variable* radius because the angle and distance between your lead arm and butt end change throughout the swing. Tour pros bend their lead arm at the elbow—by as much as 30 degrees—during their swing. A perfectly straight lead arm is an optical illusion.

You may feel like your hands, arms, and club are moving in a circle when you rotate your shoulders. But "feel isn't real." Your swing path would be circular only if your shoulders and body remained perfectly still and you stood on one leg. However, your torso mounted atop two legs shifts slightly as your shoulders rotate a diagonal axis running from your lead ear, through your sternum, and out your trailing thigh. Contrary to popular belief, your spine is not your axis of rotation.

To perform effectively, your subconscious or mind's eye needs an accurate swing map that integrates *arcs* and *straight lines*. The ideal swing model merges two different elliptical arcs. Your backswing ellipse, compared to that of your downswing ellipse, is wider and more upright. The center point or hub for each ellipse is your lead shoulder. Thus, your swing radius is a *straight line* that extends from the lead shoulder to the clubhead. *Variable* radii throughout your swing create problems.

Imagine swinging a ball on a string. The fixed radius—or *straightness*—of the string allows the ball to orbit in a tight circle. However, your golf swing is not a tight circle with a fixed radius. The swing consists of two ellipses with variable radii.

Solid contact is a function of your ability to establish a "radius of power"—a relatively straight line extending from your lead shoulder to the clubhead at impact.

How do you do that? First, shorten your swing to minimize variable radii. Second, keep your hands ahead of the clubhead and create *forward shaft lean* at impact. Third, move your hands behind your torso. Fourth, form a triangle with your forearms and chest—whereby you soften and bend your lead arm slightly at the elbow and point your elbows downward (i.e., no iron-bar lead arm). Fifth, raise your lead shoulder (i.e., swing hub) and keep rotating your hips and shoulders into impact. When you elevate and bring your lead shoulder *around the corner* at impact, you'll create a straight and powerful radius.

The human body can't create a perfectly concentric swing path because of the variability in the three-directional movement of your club, arms, and hands. Don't envision your swing as a perfect circle—but as two slightly different ellipses.

An elliptical swing compared to a circular swing generates more speed and power. Your clubhead is like a NASCAR speeding around an elliptical track. If a clubhead or NASCAR travelled on a circular track, it couldn't travel as fast. Runners, thoroughbreds, and race cars use oval tracks. The Milkway spirals elliptically. The earth orbits elliptically. And fitness training equipment moves elliptically.

Imagine your clubhead as a satellite traveling in an elliptical orbit. The velocity of the satellite will vary depending on its orbital location. A satellite moves fastest at its orbital lowpoint (i.e., when it's closest to the Earth and when gravitational forces are the strongest). In your elliptical golf swing, your clubhead also moves fastest when your arms—employing centripetal force—are closest to your body at the swing's low point.

If you envision your club path as a perfect circle, you invite problems. A circular club path invites a matching backswing and downswing. No way! Your backswing and downswing paths don't match. Your backswing plane tends to be more upright, and your downswing plane tends to be flatter.

Furthermore, your swing is not one continuous motion. Rather, it's a discontinuous ellipse. It moves imperceptively in a "go-stop-go" sequence. Your backswing, in other words, must stop momentarily at the top to change directions. Only UFOs can reverse directions without stopping. Suppose your car slams into a snow bank. To extricate your car, you must reverse gears. However, you can't reverse gears until your car stops moving forward. In other words, extricating your car from a snow bank demands *discontinuous* movement.

If you mistakenly envision your swing path as a *continuous* circle or ellipse, such as a whirling carousel or ferris wheel, you're ignoring your transition. Program your thinking to stop momentarily at the top to reverse directions.

Actually, the swing plane is slightly bowed, not flat. Therefore, imagine that the tips of your thumbs are tracing a curved swing path. Or imagine that you're swinging a club with a flexible hickory shaft rather than with a rigid steel shaft. Flexible hickory shafts more closely resemble *whips*. Rigid steel shafts more closely resemble *levers*. Whipping actions move rapidly. Leveraging actions move slowly.

There's another key ellipse hidden in your swing. Your trailing elbow—similar to that of submarine pitcher in baseball or an underhand pitcher in softball—forms an elliptical path into the impact zone. The cup or inside of your trailing elbow points skyward as it moves through the hitting area. The elliptical motion of the trailing elbow in the downswing is akin to that of skipping a stone across a pond. Moe Norman used the term "sunnyside up" to denote the elliptical path of the trailing elbow at impact.

The quality of your ball-striking depends on how quickly in your downswing you can rotate your navel (i.e., center-of-mass) to unleash the latent power in your hips, pelvis, thighs, and legs.

Suppose you want to punch your moronic boss in the face. You need to retract your right arm and fist like a piston in a straight line to generate linear forces. Obviously, you have to rotate your hips and shoulders in the process. However, your brain can't hold two thoughts simultaneously. Therefore, focus on what's most important: delivering a straight and powerful punch.

The linear and powerful forces used in delivering a punch also apply to your golf swing. To create a flat spot for your driver as it approaches impact, position the ball farther forward in your stance and assume some rear axis tilt at address. As your torso rotates into impact when using your driver, focus on creating a flat spot—before and after the ball—to generate linear forces with your arms and club shaft.

In many respects, hitting a golf ball is like hammering a nail. When you're hammering a nail, your main goal is to hammer the nail *straight*. Thus, your brain must momentarily focus on straight lines—not arcs. I'm not saying that you shouldn't swing the hammer along an arc. I'm saying that you must also pound the nail *straight*.

Your brain can't hold circles and lines simultaneously. Therefore, focus mostly on the circle. Using your lead shoulder, swing the butt end in a tilted circle that passes *under* your Adam's apple *over* the base of your neck (i.e., 7th vertebrae of your cervical spine).

Rebellious Discernment

Most bewildered golfers seek expert advice. Presumably, experts can process complex and technical information more effectively than you can. Deluged by numerous, varied, and contradictory swing theories, golfers seek parental-like authorities to tell them what to do and how to do it. However, there are serious consequences associated with seeking expert advice.

Consider what happened to Tiger Woods. After six coaches, roughly five swing changes, and four back surgeries, Woods hit the skids before he finally decided to go it alone. Swing changes, especially rapid and dramatic ones, induce new stresses and strains on your muscles, ligaments, tendons, joints, and spine.

In January 2018, Woods stated, "The only big deal about it is that no one really understands what it's like to have a fused back and be able to play. It's not about how the swing actually looks like. You can get into positions and things of that nature, and there are a lot of things I can't do anymore because of the nature of the fusion. So I'm relying on feel and my past performances." In September 2018 with no coach by his side, Tiger Woods won the Tour Players Championship in Atlanta.

Ben Hogan, who had few mentors, believed that a swing coach was a crutch. Hogan was fiercely independent.

Possessing a genius-level IQ, Hogan trusted his instincts. Henry Picard did offer Hogan tips on occasion. However, Picard was a trusted friend, not a coach.

Today, befuddled golfers are addicted to expert advice. We have become enamored with the intellect, experience, status, and self-assurance of experts who emit the most sparks. Hence, we overestimate the judgments of others and underestimate our own. Consequently, we subordinate our reasoning and decision making to suit the wisdom and certainty of others.

When you relinquish your decision-making powers to so-called experts, you unknowingly shut down your brain. The neurological effect of exposing your brain to expert advice has been evidenced in brain scans. Dr. David Freedman, a University of Chicago neurobiologist who authored *Wrong: Why Experts Keep Failing Us and How to Know When Not to Trust Them* (2010), asserts that the brain shuts down slightly when you receive expert advice.

Using an MRI machine, Freedman scanned the brains of adults as they listened to the voices of experts expound on a range of topics. When subjects received expert advice, they switched off their brain's decision making and critical thinking faculties. When you listen to experts impart advice, your brain flat-lines, and you become vulnerable to exploitation.

Freedman asserts (1) that as much as 90 percent of advice imparted by physicians has been found to be substantially or completely incorrect, (2) that there's a 1-in-12 chance that your doctor has incorrectly diagnosed your condition, (3) that professionally prepared tax returns are more likely to contain more errors than self-prepared returns, and (4) that half of all newspaper articles contain at least one factual error.

A recent article in the *Journal of American Medical Association* discussed how expert surgeons removed healthy ovaries and operated on the wrong side of a patient's body.

Another article discussed how expert physicians, when they observe CT scans, often see only what they expect to see. Experienced radiologists, for example, looking at the scan of a pneumonia patient's lungs will often overlook a tumor situated only three inches away. If experienced, competent, and intelligent physicians can make mistakes, so can experienced golf gurus.

Experts make mistakes every day. Consider how your game has languished because you blindly accepted half-ass advice. To enhance your skill sets, keep the decision-making part of your brain switched on. I'm aware of the irony here: I'm giving you advice about the dangers of taking advice. Learning is a two-way street: *Learn how to learn* and *Learn to doubt what you learn*.

In his book *On Being Certain* (2009), Dr. Robert Burton claims that *certainty*—the feeling of being right even when you're wrong—is an involuntary brain mechanism independent of reason and conscious choice. Placing utter confidence in the knowledge of others is a potentially dangerous mental flaw. To escape indecision, confusion, and information overload, golfers take refuge in absolute ideologies. Take a nuanced approach—not an absolute approach—to what you're thinking and learning. Understanding and assessing how your mind and brain function will mitigate your certainty bias. View know-it-all instructors who ooze confidence and certainty with respect mingled with suspicion.

To expand your learning, consider PGA- and non-PGA-certified instructors. There are many phenomenal instructors who have no affiliation with the PGA. Just because instructors have three letters after their name doesn't make them great teachers. Today, many PGA instructors teach incorrect ball flight laws. Your ideal golf instructor must understand how your mind, brain, body, and swing function.

The old adage "you get what your pay for" doesn't necessarily apply to golf instruction. Many expensive private lessons from PGA instructors are worthless. Conversely, many free lessons from amateur instructors on YouTube are priceless. Find a certified or noncertified instructor—online, at a club, or at a Tin Cup driving range—capable of diagnosing your flaws, simplifying the complex, making the strange familiar, and fostering rapid growth.

Ben Hogan said, "Reverse every natural instinct and do the opposite of what you're inclined to do, and you'll come very close to having a perfect golf swing." When I reversed my thinking and focused on swinging the *butt* end, rather than the *clubhead*, I experienced one of my greatest breakthroughs. Great golfers, whether they're aware of it or not, are actually swinging the *butt end*. I clearly observed Ben Hogan and Moe Norman doing it. And that's good enough for me.

Switch on your brain by exercising *rebellious discernment*. If you want to achieve a breakthrough, allow varied, competing, and contradictory opinions battle it out. Weigh, consider, challenge, and test new, diverse, and radical golf advice. Embrace uncertainty. When I challenged the conventional practice of rotating around the axis of my spine, I experienced one of my biggest breakthroughs. *Now I tilt and rotate my shoulders to swing my arms.* The rocking motion of shoulders engages my lower body, powers my torso, and swings my arms. In fact, I trigger my swing by lowering my lead shoulder.

The French novelist Stendhal claimed that in every successful relationship there is always a healthy measure of doubt. Doubt endows each moment with desire and anticipation. A successful relationship with golf must also include a healthy measure of doubt.

When you consider the advice of golf experts, ask yourself several key questions: *How will the components associated with this change systemically affect other components? Which assumptions underpin this advice? What additional evidence supports this advice? Which factors does this advice ignore? Does this advice fit my specific needs, goals, and circumstances?*

Growth occurs when the risk of remaining closed becomes more painful and perilous than the risk of making changes. Vulnerability drives improvement. Einstein wrote, "In the middle of difficulty lies opportunity."

Seek the advice of expert teachers. Realize, however, that there's no ideal and definitive method for learning and teaching the golf swing. The swing is a quandary on par with reversing the aging process, turning lead into gold, or creating a perpetual motion machine.

Optical Illusions

In 1915, William Ely Hill published his famous optical illusion sketch titled "My Wife and My Mother-in-Law" in *Puck* magazine. The shaded sketch, depending on how you perceive it, depicts either a young girl or an old hag. The sketch was accompanied by the following caption: "They are both in this picture. Find them."

In 1930, Edwin Boring, a psychologist researching optical illusions and perceptions, wrote a scientific paper on Hill's sketch. Boring considered Hill's sketch the quintessential optical illusion, since no clear lines separate the two figures.

Perception is the state or process of gaining awareness through your senses. Optical illusions seamlessly and constantly shift your perceptions from one object to another. You realize that there are two figures in Hill's sketch; however, you can see only one at a time. That's because your brain is incapable of perceiving two images simultaneously. Hence, you must train your brain to recognize two separate patterns.

Viewed from a golf perspective, optical illusions teach you two key things: perceptions permeate your eyes and brain AND perceptions are active modes of awareness. Optical illusions make discerning truth very difficult.

PGA instructors Steven Bann and Jim Waldron claim that illusive arm movements represent golf's greatest optical illusion. Reportedly, most golfers fail to perceive the dimensional distortion or optical illusion associated with how the arms move in the golf swing. Most golfers, deceived by two-dimensional images derived from videos and photographs, wrongly assume that Tour pros swing their arms sideways, across their chest, and around their spine. Golfers, whether they're aware of it, are brainwashed.

According to Jim Waldron, the movement of your arms sideways and across the chest is an optical illusion. Waldron claims that your arms are not moving independently. Your arms—attached at your shoulder joints—are being moved by your torso. Your hypermobile shoulder joints, which rock, slide, and glide, move your arms and hands in concert with your swing's kinetic chain.

Tour pros are actually multitasking. When Tour pros connect their arms to their torso, they seamlessly blend two different motions at two different speeds. In sum, Tour pros don't swing their arms *independently*. Their rotating torso flings their passive arms like loose straps. When they rotate their torso at 30 mph, they swing their arms into impact at 70 mph. Multitasking—merging different motions at different speeds—greatly complicates your brain's ability to understand and master swing mechanics.

Jim Waldron, a brilliant instructor, considers the arm swing illusion the "cancer of the golf swing." Golfers, imprisoned by this optical illusion, continue to move their arms sideways and around their body. Essentially, the golf swing is a high-speed optical illusion.

The rotation of their torso obscures the fact that Tour pros are *vertically* lifting their hands and arms. To invert and stand up the club, your hands and arms must move vertically. Swinging your arms sideways and your club on a low, flat arc—flowing from an optical illusion in your swing's high-speed, complex system—causes serious problems.

To master the swing, you must understand the cognitive nature of optical illusions. More specifically, you must understand how visual distortions entice the brain to make false assumptions and induce errant behaviors.

Psychologists studying optical illusions once asked thousands of subjects to estimate the average length of highway dashes. Most subjects estimated that the lane dividers on most highways were only two feet long. Actually, most highway dashes are between 10 and 15 feet long. Here's the takeaway: When things operate at high speed, as in a speeding car or in a swing with the clubhead moving at 90 mph, optical illusions take root and your brain makes false assumptions.

To recognize an optical illusion and draw logical conclusions, you must slow things down to engage "executive functioning"—the process occurring in your brain's frontal cortex that sharpens learning, adjusts thinking, makes decisions, and nourishes awareness.

You don't need "executive functioning" to drink a beer or wash your car. However, you need "executive functioning" to understand and access complex and nuanced swing mechanics.

If you're not improving, ask yourself: *What will it take to convince me that my previous assumptions and actions about the golf swing are dead wrong?* Susana Martinez-Conde, Director of the Laboratory of Visual Neuroscience at Barrow Neurological Institute in Phoenix, Arizona, defines an illusion as a phenomenon in which our subjective perception doesn't match the physical reality of the world.

In their article "Misperceptions" (*Natural History Magazine*), Susana Martinez-Conde and Stephen Macknik assert that the brain has a limited number of neurons, wires, and neuronal connections, "So in some cases, illusions may be due to the brain's need to take shortcuts." Simply put, your lazy brain has a tendency to hastily attach more importance to certain features in your visual landscapes than to others.

The swing's illusionary nature invites shortcuts, fuzzy thinking, and errant behaviors. In fact, noted neuroscientists suggest that you can fast-track and sharpen your powers of "executive functioning" by studying how magic tricks and optical illusions manipulate and distort your perceptions, thoughts, and behaviors. Do you see where I'm going with this?

"The Spinning Dancer" is a famous video of an optical illusion created by Nobuyuki Kayahara in 2003. It features a distorted and two-dimensional silhouette of a pirouetting ballerina. Most people wrongly perceive the dancer to be spinning clockwise or counterclockwise depending on whether they focus on the dancer's left or right pivot foot. Actually, the dancer in this two-dimensional animation isn't *spinning*. She's actually *shifting* from side to side. Distorted visual feedback in the brain creates the illusion that the dancer is spinning.

The brain gets tricked when it superimposes a false three-dimensional reality on a two-dimensional image. In sum, distortions of dimensional depth induce false assumptions. Dimensional-depth distortions of brief duration that operate at high speed trick you into believing that Tour pros are swinging their arms sideways, across their chest, and around their spine—instead of in front of their torso.

To understand a golf swing or a magic trick, you must slow it down. Einstein wrote, "Look deep into nature, and you will understand everything better."

Optical illusions, like Hill's sketch, Kayahara's spinning dancer, and Jim Waldron's and Steve Bann's left arm movement, occur when your brain distorts dimensional depth, takes shortcuts, and misinterprets visual stimuli.

When you view Hill's sketch, you invariably perceive the haggy mother-in-law—never the attractive girl. Last week you also perceived your mother-in-law when your friend Ronnie, a functional psychopath, showed you his new snake tattoo.

The Follow-through

Most stymied golfers ignore the following advice stressed by the best players and coaches: "Finish your swing with a proper follow-through."

For years, instructors have urged golfers to assume a theatrical pose in their follow-through. However, most golfers ignore this advice. Why hold your follow-through? You've already made contact with the ball. What's the point? Plus, you resent golfers who hold their follow-through to display their grandeur. Why does your follow-through, the residue of your swing, matter?

If you've dismissed the role of the follow-through in your swing, listen to what neuroscientists maintain. University of Cambridge scientists assert that elite performers in target-oriented activities such as golf, tennis, bowling, softball, darts, and horseshoes always finish with the correct follow-through. Your follow-through, in fact, may be the most important phase of your golf swing.

The muscle contractions created in your follow-through leave valuable and lasting motor-memory traces in your brain. In brief, a proper and deliberative follow-through not only completes your *existing* swing, but also produces a subconscious neural blueprint or motor-memory for your *next* swing.

In the golf swing, an exquisitely timed movement lasting only 1.4 seconds and involving 600 muscles demands a proper and graceful follow-through to prevent injury and terminate the swinging motion.

Researchers Ian Howard, David Franklin, and Daniel Wolpert in "The Value of the Follow-Through Derives from Motor Learning Depending on Future Actions" (*Current Biology*) suggest that athletes employing a proper and consistent follow-through experience accelerated learning. You'll learn swing mechanics faster by employing a consistent and repetitive follow-through.

Using different follow-throughs, thereby introducing variability (what neuroscientists call *noise* or *interference patterns* in your muscles), retards learning. Researchers do not prescribe a specific follow-through for all golfers. They recommend that golfers or any target-oriented athletes trying to master a complex skill should constantly rehearse a proper, consistent, nuanced, and biomechanically correct follow-through.

These authors state, "In ball sports, we are taught to follow through, despite the inability of events after contact or release to influence the outcome. Here we show that the specific motor memory active at any given moment critically depends on the movement that will be made in the near future. . . . This implies that when learning a skill, a variable follow-through would activate multiple motor memories across practice, whereas a consistent follow-through would activate a single motor memory, resulting in faster learning."

Here's the bottom line: poor swings invariably flow from flawed sensory input, inept planning, and variable muscular responses. In sum, each time you swing, no matter how hard you try, your swing will be slightly different. Therefore, why confuse matters by employing random and different follow-throughs every time you swing?

To release the club and shift your weight in your follow-through, employ a variation of Nick Faldo's "elbow whip." In your follow-through, not only whip your lead elbow, but also counterrotate your upper lead arm and adduct your left shoulder (i.e., move your shoulder blade away from your spine). Activate your left side in your follow-through.

Imagine yourself freewheeling your hands and arms over your lead shoulder as if you were hurling an Olympic discus or hammer.

Use a mirror to rehearse the follow-throughs of elite golfers who share your unique parameters. Hold a proper and consistent follow-through for several seconds every time you swing.

To ensure a correct follow-through, rotate your hips only 45 degrees in your backswing. To transfer your weight in your downswing, rotate your trailing knee 120 degrees; rapidly turn your navel, trailing hip and pelvis toward the target; swivel your trailing ankle counterclockwise; and toe-drag your trailing foot. The more rapidly you thrust your navel, trailing hip and pelvis "around the corner" in your follow-through, the more power you produce.

The next time your brother-in-law stops over for a free breakfast and asks why you're making that weird pivoting motion when you're flipping pancakes, tell him that you're working on your follow-through.

Less Is More

Mario firmly believes *more is better*. That's why he tightens his grip, lengthens his backswing, maximizes his pelvic rotation, hastens his tempo, optimizes his lateral shift, and hits five jumbo buckets every time he goes to Marty's Hack Land.

Mario eats at Johnny's Italian Rendezvous, despite their lousy clam sauce, because the portions are huge; drinks Brew Meister *Armageddon*, despite its skunky taste, because of its high alcohol content; and drives a 2017 Dodge Challenger (a.k.a. his *Ass Rocket*) because it has a 485-horsepower engine. Mario says, "Anyone who thinks *less is more* is an ass-hat."

To improve dramatically, consider adopting a *less is more* mentality. When you simplify and abbreviate your swing, you eliminate excess movement, enhance your balance, increase your power, refine your timing, hold your posture, make better contact, increase your consistency, and minimize injuries. A shorter swing is tighter and better.

To synchronize and connect your arms and torso, shorten your backswing. At address, imagine that you're facing 12 on a clock. When you're hitting short irons, stop your backswing when your hands reach the 3 o'clock position. When you're hitting mid-irons, stop your backswing when your hands reach the 4 o'clock position. When you're hitting woods, stop your backswing when your hands reach the 5 o'clock position. Educate your hands to assume these three positions. Hogan's hand position for every backswing was club-specific: *3 o'clock, 4 o'clock, 5 o'clock* . . . stop.

"Any intelligent fool can make things bigger and more complex," Einstein wrote, "It takes a touch of genius and a lot of courage to move in the opposite direction."

When you simplify your swing, things tend to happen naturally and effortlessly. *The 80/20 Rule*, practiced by highly successful people, supports the concept that *less is more*. Vilfredo Pareto, an Italian economist, formulated his "80/20 Rule" when he observed that 20 percent of the peapods in his garden produced 80 percent of the peas. When Pareto later studied land ownership in England and Italy, he discovered that 20 percent of the population owned 80 percent of the land.

In 1896, Pareto, then a professor at Lausanne University, published his famous treatise "A Lesson in Political Economics." Pareto postulated that 20 percent of all causes produce 80 percent of all effects. Years later, Joseph Juran, a management consultant, dubbed this concept "The Pareto Principle" or "The 80/20 Rule.

Richard Koch, in his *The 80/20 Principle: The Secret to Achieving More with Less* (1999), explains how successful people and organizations leverage the 80/20 Rule. To achieve an 80 percent success level, according to Koch, simply identify and focus on the top 20 percent of all factors. The corollary to Koch's advice is equally important: Don't waste 80 percent of your time and energy on the wrong things.

Consider the following 80/20 statistics derived from leading corporations:

- 80 percent of a firm's business flows comes from 20 percent of its customers.

- 20 percent of a firm's products and services generate 80 percent of its profits.
- 80 percent of a firm's consumer complaints originate from 20 percent of its problems.
- 20 percent of a manager's effort and time achieve 80 percent of all meaningful results.
- 80 percent of a firm's losses flow from 20 percent of all causes.
- 20 percent of a firm's personnel generate 80 percent of its productivity.
- 80 percent of a firm's value is generated by 20 percent of its processes.

Management guru Peter Drucker said, "There is nothing quite so useless as doing with great efficiency something that should not be done at all." In his book *On the Profession of Management* (1998), Drucker discussed the relationship among three key concepts: *abandonment, concentration,* and *The 80/20 Rule.*

Abandonment denotes dumping unproductive and obsolete principles and practices. *Concentration* denotes focusing on productive and profitable principles and tasks. *The 80/20 Rule* denotes getting an 80 percent return on 20 percent of your efforts. Golfers, take heed.

In his article "Live The 80/20 Rule," Marc Winn writes, "The common approach to business is to squeeze every last drop out of each opportunity, to go 100 percent all-out, without consideration of the impact on time, productivity and wastage. . . . Spend 80 percent of your time doing the 20 percent that really gets you results. . . . It's not just about working smarter—it's about working smarter on the right things that will get you the best results."

If your game isn't improving, determine how you can work smarter—not longer and harder.

In *The 4-Hour Body* (2011), Tim Ferriss introduces his concept of "The Minimum Effective Dose" (MED), or the smallest dose needed to produce the desired outcome. He applies the MED concept for clients to achieve more in the areas of diet, fitness, cooking, etc., by doing less.

To illustrate the futility of overworking key tasks, Ferriss writes, "To boil water, the Minimum Effect Dose is 212°F (100°C) at standard air pressure. Boiled is boiled. Higher temperatures will not make it *more boiled.* Higher temperatures just consume more resources that could be used for something else more productive."

Golfers should invoke The Minimum Effective Dose by focusing on what matters most, by assessing your progress, and by optimizing your time and effort. If you're not progressing, stop deluding yourself. Ferris writes, "Anything beyond the Minimum Effective Dose is wasteful."

Throughout his book, Ferriss stresses learning how to learn. Accordingly, Ferriss recommends several strategies to enhance your learning. First, *create a feedback loop*—from yourself and others—to spot your errors and identify specific areas of improvement. Consult what Ferriss calls a "mastermind group" to acquire expert advice on deconstructed and problematic areas of your swing. In addition, monitor and measure self-generated feedback.

Second, *employ deliberate and focused practice* for a relatively short period of time. Ferriss—who bases his metalearning techniques on Ericcson's theory of deliberate practice extrapolated from the routines of elite athletes, musicians, and writers—recommends concentrating on very specific skills. Progress doesn't proceed in leaps and bounds. It happens slowly and incrementally.

Third, *become a teacher.* To improve your skill sets, teach others exactly what you're trying to learn yourself. Einstein wrote, "If you can't explain it to a six-year old, you don't understand it yourself." Teaching others obliges you to simplify and clarify complex ideas. When you teach others, you assume the responsibility and motivation to learn pertinent information and understand what you're saying and doing.

To improve your skills, apply two key economic principles: "Opportunity Costs" and "The Law of Diminishing Returns." When you use your time and effort effectively, you'll achieve *productive returns*. When you use your time and effort ineffectively, you'll achieve *diminishing returns*. When you waste your time and effort, you'll achieve *negative returns*. The fact that most golfers, despite their extensive efforts, have not lowered their handicaps in decades suggests they're spending their time unproductively.

Invoke The Minimum Effective Dose Rule by focusing on the *common denominators* in the swings of all elite golfers, namely, balance, rhythm, and tempo. Also, learn the correct takeaway and follow-through. Most important, understand that *less is more*.

To simplify your thinking and energize your swing, employ Homer Kelley's famous, but widely misunderstood, concept of the "flying wedges." In *The Golfing Machine* (1971), Kelley explains the formation and function of the *left arm flying wedge* and the *right forearm flying wedge*. Let me explain.

To form these flying wedges at address, you must point the butt of the club at your navel, position the club toe-up on the ground, and assume the correct grip, posture, and stance.

The *left arm flying wedge* consists of the following *vertical* members: (1) a line extending from your left shoulder to your left wrist, (2) a line extending from your left wrist—running down the shaft—to the sweet spot, and (3) a line extending from the sweet spot back to your left shoulder. These members form a vertical triangle—akin to a sail—that opens and closes like a fan as your left wrist hinges and unhinges.

The *right forearm flying wedge* consists of the following *horizontal* members: (1) a line extending from your right elbow—running along the back of your right forearm—to the back of your bent right wrist, (2) a line extending from the back of your bent right wrist to the pressure point on your trigger that pushes against the grip, and (3) a line extending from your trigger finger back to your right elbow.

The "flying wedges"—the left vertical and the right horizontal—must remain at right angles to each other. When you properly employ Kelley's "flying wedges," (1) you'll understand why your left hand must grip the club in your fingers and your right hand must grip the club across your palm, (2) you'll bow your left wrist and flex your right, (3) you'll create the requisite forward shaft lean, (4) you'll use the pressure point in your trigger finger to execute a powerful palm strike, and (5) you'll unleash the immense power and magic residing in your right elbow.

In *Wind, Sand and Stars* (1939), Antoine de Saint-Exupéry writes, "There is an ancient myth about an image asleep in a bock of marble until it is carefully disengaged by the sculptor. The sculptor must himself feel that he is not so much inventing or sculpturing the curve of the breast or shoulder as delivering the image from its prison."

You'll achieve your ideal golf swing—not when you have nothing more to *add*—but when you have nothing more to *subtract*.

Fleeting Indicators

Fleeting indicators are subtle and evanescent bits of sonar data monitored and assessed by astute submarine commanders to detect the presence of enemy submarines. Submarine commanders, schooled in sophisticated information-management techniques, are adept at processing, filtering, and responding to a wide range of fleeting indicators.

Golf's fleeting indicators—cryptic data-bits in the words and images of DVDs, videos, photos, books, and articles—also appear on your brain's sonar scope. Like savvy submarine commanders, you must have the vigilance, perspicacity, and intelligence to recognize and interpret obscure signals. Unfortunately, stymied golfers tend to suffer from situation blindness.

Fleeting indicators have greatly improved my putting stroke. Acceleration is the most important principle in the putting stroke. Fleeting indicators among the putting strokes of expert golfers have taught me to employ a *very abbreviated and slow* back stroke—combined with a very *abbreviated and accelerated* forward stroke.

Abbreviate your slow back stroke to exert the least amount of acceleration in your forward stroke to roll the ball just beyond the cup. I use this "pop-stroke" technique to eliminate three-putting.

Recently, fleeting indicators appeared on my sonar scope when I watched Phil Mickelson putt during a televised Tour event. The commentators mentioned that Mickelson, who was struggling with his putting, recently received a putting lesson from Dave Stockton, Sr. The television analysts, showing before-and-after video footage of Phil's putting, discussed and demonstrated recent changes in Phil's technique. Adopting Stockton's advice, Phil made several changes that have paid off.

New Grip: Before, Phil would overlap the index finger of his lead hand over the knuckles of his trail hand, thereby creating undue tension running up his lead arm. Now, Phil crooks his (previously straight) index finger so it doesn't overlap as much, thereby allowing him to execute a smooth takeaway. No more tension.

New Preputt Routine: Before, Phil would stare at the hole while he took six or seven practice strokes. Now, Phil stares at the hole for approximately ten seconds, takes his stance, then rivets his focus on rolling the ball with the proper speed, distance, and direction. Stockton's advice is consonant with what leading sports physiologists postulate about "quiet-eye" movements.

Mark Smith, a sports performance researcher at The University of Lincoln in Great Britain, submits that you should narrow your focus to the putter and ball (not the cup) for a brief period immediately preceding the takeaway.

New Stance: Before Phil assumed a very narrow stance, opened his lead foot slightly, and squared his trail foot. Now, Phil assumes a wider stance and squares up both feet, thereby allowing him to putt across his body and achieve better balance.

Inexplicably, the commentators ignored what seemed to be the most obvious and important before-and-after change in

Phil's putting: *His Forward Press.* In Phil's new putting style, he sets up with his hands directly over the ball, then slides his hands one or two inches toward the target by slightly bowing his lead wrist.

On the practice green, I quickly applied a precious fleeting indicator—the subtle forward press and bowing of the lead wrist that Phil introduced in his putting stroke. Accordingly, I nudged my hands toward the target for one or two inches, bowed my lead wrist slightly, and focused on a smooth ball takeaway. Eureka. It worked like a charm.

Sam Snead in *Better Golf the Sam Snead Way* (1989) wrote, "For my money, the single most important device for getting nerves and muscles ready to execute the golf swing properly is the forward press. I've never made a golf swing that did not start from a forward press, and I've never met a golfer who failed to play better after learning to trigger his swing this way."

The action inherent in using a buggy whip, namely moving the butt end slightly forward before moving it backward, applies directly to both the putting stroke and full swing. Before moving the club backward, to execute a fluid motion, you must move it slightly forward.

Using a forward press and bowing my lead wrist slightly—a subtle micromove—allowed me to take the clubhead away smoothly, unify both hands, steady the putter face, roll the ball fluidly, and establish a rhythmic stroke. Insignificant changes can induce startling results.

The forward press, a trivial and subtle movement, assumes little relevance in the imaginations of most golfers. However, the forward press is exceedingly important. Avoid *groupthink*. Find your own hidden treasures. If you look deeply for jewels hidden in the swings of professionals, your perspicacity will be rewarded.

One of my biggest putting breakthroughs occurred when I opened the putter face one degree at address, thereby setting the heel slightly ahead of the toe. Opening the putter face compensates for the rotation that invariably occurs when you try to keep the face square, straight back and through. I shifted the center of rotation from the putter head to my hands.

The golf swing consists of countless, spontaneous, magical, hidden, and subtle facets. To sharpen your wits and revolutionize your thinking, search for fleeting indicators. The golf swing, like a prowling enemy submarine, is hidden from view. The dynamic, holistic, and rapid interaction of innumerable moving parts, lasting only 1.4 seconds, makes the swing extremely difficult to understand, diagnose, and correct.

You don't need a Raytheon AN/AQS-20 sonar system to detect fleeting indicators in an ocean of golf information. Your brain has its own sonar system. Just switch it on. When you start amassing fleeting indicators and hidden secrets, you'll start playing D.I.Y.G. (Do-It-Yourself Golf).

References

Abresman, S. (2012). *The half-life of facts: Why everything we know has an expiration date.* New York: Penguin Books.

Adams, A., Hartnett, E., & Clough, G. (2015). "Turn it on its head! Juxtaposed learning." http://oro.open.ac.uk/44758/1/AdamsHartnettClough2015%20Juxtaposed%20learning.

Anderson, M. (2010). "Neural reuse: A fundamental organizational principle of the brain." *Behavioral and Brain Sciences. 33,* 245–313.

Aumann, M. (2015, March 9). "Golf tip: When it's ok to throw your clubs." Retrieved from https://www.pga.com/news/lesson-learned/throwing-clubs-golf-drill-when-its-ok-throw-clubs.

Beall, J. (2017, June 26). "Do it yourself: swings." *Golf Digest.* Retrieved from https://www.golfdigesrt.com/story/do-it-yourself-swings.

Becoming an expert takes more than practice. (July 2, 2014). Association for Psychological Research. Retrieved from https://www.psychologicalscience.org/news/releases/becoming-an-expert-takes-more-than-practice.html.

Beilock, S. (2011). *Choke: What the secrets of the brain reveal about getting it right when you have to.* New York: Atria Books.

Blakeslee, S. (2006, Jan.10). "Cells that read minds." *The New York Times.* Retrieved from http://www.nytimes.com/2006/01/10/science/cells-that-read-minds.html.

Boomer, P. (1946). *On Learning Golf: A Valuable Guide to Better Golf.* New York: Alfred A. Knopf

Bradberry, T. (2005, Nov.). "8 Ways smart people act stupid." Retrieved from https://www.linkedin.com/pulse/why-smart-people-act-so-stupid-dr-travis-bradberry

Bradley, N. (2013). *Kinetic golf: Picture the game like never before.* New York: Abrams.

Burke, J., Nelson, B., Runyan, P., et al. (1963). *How to solve your golf problems.* New York: Grosset & Dunlap.

Burton, R. (2009). *On being certain: Believing you're right even when you're not.* New York: St. Martin's Griffin.

Carr, T. (2017, August). "Too many meds? America's love affair with prescription drugs." *Consumer Reports.* Retrieved from https://www.consumerreports.org/prescription-drugs/too-many-meds-americas-love-affair-with-prescription-medication/.

Churchland, M.M., Afshar, A., & Shenoy, K.V. (2006, Dec.). "A central source of movement variability." *Neuron.* 6, 1085–1096.

Crossley, M., Ashby, F., & Maddox, W. (Aug., 2013). "Erasing the engram: The unlearning of procedural skills." *Journal of Experimental Psychology.* 142(3).

Danziger, S., Levay, J., & Avnaim-Pesso, L. (2011, Apr.). "Extraneous factors in judicial decisions." *Proceedings of the National Academy of Sciences.* 108(17), 6889–6892.

de Saint-Exupery, A. (1939). *Wind, sand and stars.* New York: Harcourt Brace.

de la Torre, M. (2014). *Understanding the golf swing.* New York: Skyhorse.

Diamond, A. (2013). "Executive functions." *Annual Review of Psychology.* 64. 135–168.

Di Domenico SI, & Ryan, RM. "The Emerging Neuroscience of Intrinsic Motivation: A New Frontier in Self-Determination Research." *Frontiers of Human Neuroscience.* 2017;11:145. Published 2017, Mar 24. doi:10.3389/fnhum.2017.00145 Retreived from https://www.ncbi.nlm.nih.gov/pmc/articles/PMC5364176/#B19

D'Innocenzo, G., Gonzalez, C., Williams, M., & Bishop, D. (2016, May). "Looking to learn: The effects of visual guidance on observational learning of the golf swing." Retrieved from http://journals.plos.org/plosone/article?id=10.1371/journal.pone.0155442.

Doidge, Norman. (2007). *The brain that changes itself.* New York: Viking.

Ericsson, A., Krampe, R., & Tesch-Romer, C. (1993). "The role of deliberate practice in the acquisition of expert performance." *Psychological Review.* 100(3). 363–406.

Eriksson, P., Perfilieva, E., Bjork, E.T., Alborn, A., Nordborg, C., Peterson, A., & Gage, F. (1998, Nov.). "Neurogenesis in the adult hippocampus." *Nature Medicine.* Retrieved from http://highexistence.com/boost-brain-harnessing-neurogenesis/.

Ferdindands, R. (2004). "Golf swing mechanics: The path to the future golf swing." Retrieved from Archives of The International Conference of The Society of Biomechanics in Sport website: http://ojs.ub.uni-konstsanz de/cpa.article/view/1298.

References

Fitts, P., & Posner, M. (1979). *Human performance*. Santa Barbara, CA: Praeger.

Flick, J. (1997). *On golf: Lessons from America's master teacher*. New York: Villard Books.

Funahashi, S., & Andreau, J.M. (2013, Dec.). "Prefrontal cortex and neural mechanisms of executive function." *Journal of Phsiology-Paris. 107*(6). 471–482.

Gibson, R. (1998). *Rethinking the future*. Boston: Nicholas Brealey.

Gladwell, M. (2008). *Outliers*. New York: Little, Brown.

Goldberg, E. (2009). *The New executive brain: Frontal cortex in a complex world*. New York: Oxford University Press.

Gordon, B. (2014, Jan.) "Delayed gratification: A battle that must be won." Retrieved from www.psychologytoday.com/blog/obesely-speaking/201401 /delayed-gratification-battle-must-be-won.

Gnau, S. (2013, Sept.). "Putting big data into context." Retrieved from https://www.wired.com/insights/2013/09/putting-big-data-in-context/.

Grafton, S. (2009). "What can dance teach us about learning?" Retrieved from www.dana.org/What_Can_Dance_Teach_Us_about_Learning_/.

Heath, E. (2018, Feb.). "10 tour pro ball striking tips." *GolfMonthly*. Retrieved from https://www.golf-monthly.co.uk/tips/10-tour-pro-ball-striking-tips-151083.

Herrigel, E. (1991). *Zen in the art of archery*. New York: Random House.

Heshmat, S. (2016, June). "10 Reasons we rush for immediate gratification." Retrieved From https://www.psychologytoday.com/blog /science-choice/201606/10-reasons-we-rush-immediate-gratification.

Hogan, B. (1996). *Five lessons: The modern fundamentals of golf*. New York: Touchstone.

Huber, J. (2012). *Applying educational psychology in coaching athletes*. Champaign, IL: Kinetics.

Hussein, R. (2018, Jan.). "Functions of Dopamine: What is Dopamine and how does it affect you?" Retrieved from https://blog.cognifit /functions-of-dopamine-serve-you/.

Kelley, H. (2010). *The golf machine: The curious quest that solved golf*. New York: Avery. 7th ed.

Kirschner, P., & van Merrienboer, J. (2013). "Do learners really know best?" Urban legends in education. *Educational Psychologist. 48*:3, 169–183.

Kosslyn, S., & Miller, W. (2013). *Top brain, bottom brain: Surprising insights into how you think*. New York: Simon & Schuster.

Kosslyn, S., & Miller, W. (2014). "Are you comfortable operating in mover mode?" Retrieved from https://www.psychologytoday.com/blog/the -theory-cognitive-modes/201402/are-you-most-comfortable-operating -in-stimulator-mode.

"Know your brain: The prefrontal cortex." (Anonymous, 2014, May). Retrieved from https://www.neuroscientificallychallenged.com/blog/2014/5/16/know-your-brain-prefrontal-cortex.

Knudson, G. (1988). *The natural golf swing.* Toronto: McClelland and Stewart.

Leiterts, U. (2014, Aug.). The age of data literacy (video file). Retrieved from https://www.youtube.com/watch?v=speKlXgUTX8.

Mahadevan, L., & Venkadesan, M. (2017, Apr.). "Optimal strategies for throwing." Retrieved from https://doi.org/10.1098/rsos.170136.

Mann, R. (1998). *Swing like a pro.* New York: Broadway.

Martin, R. (2007). *The opposable mind.* Boston: Harvard Business Review.

Mason, J. (n.d.). "Why people quit golf." Retrieved from https://scpga.com/why-people-quit-golf/.

McSpadden, K. (2015, May). "You have a shorter attention span than a goldfish." Retrieved from https://time.com/3858309/attention-span.

Meister, D.W., Ladd, A.L, Butler, E.E., Zhao, B., Rogers, C.J., & Ros, J. (2011). "Rotational biomechanics of the elite golf swing: Benchmarks for amateurs." *Journal of Applied Biomechanics.* 27. 242–251.

Miller, G., Galanter, E., & Pribram, K. (1960). *The path and the structure of behavior.* New York: Holt, Rinehart & Winston.

Montoya, B.S., Brown, L.E., Coburn, J.W., & Zinder, S.M. (2009, Aug.). "Effect of warm-up with different weighted bats on normal baseball bat velocity." *Journal of Strength & Conditioning Research.* 23(5), 1566–1569.

Nelson, B. (1985). *Shape your swing the modern way.* Port Charlot, UK: Ailsa.

Netzley, M. (2016, Dec.). "What is unlearning? Unpacking one of L&D's hottestbuzzwords." Retrieved from https://www.linkedin.com/pulse/what-unlearning-unpacking-one-lds-hottest-buzzwords-netzley-ph-d-.

Orenstein, D. (2007, Jan.). "On the golf tee or the pitcher's mound, brain dooms motion to inconsistency." Retrieved from https://news.stanford.edu/https://news/2007/january17/movement-011707.html.

Parent, J. (2002). *Zen golf: mastering the mental game.* New York: Random House.

Penick, H. (1992). *Harvey Penick's little red book: Lessons and teachings from a lifetime in golf.* New York: Simon & Schuster.

Perrow, C. (1999). *Normal Accidents.* Princeton, NJ: Princeton University Press.

Picchi, A. (2014, May.). "Where have all the golfers gone?" Retrieved from https://www.cbsnews.com/news/where-have-all-the-golfers-gone/.

Pinker, S. (1997). *How the mind works.* New York: W.W. Norton & Company.

Pope, D., & Schwietzer, M. (2011, Feb.). "Is Tiger Woods loss averse? Persistent bias in the face of experience, competition and high stakes."

American Economic Review. 101(129-157). Retrieved from http://www.aeaweb.org/articles.php?doi.

Priest, D. (2016, June). "Tackling instant gratification." Retrieved from https://www.thestar.com.my/news/education/2016/06/19/tackling-instant-gratification/.

Ramachandran, V.S. (2012). *The tell-tale brain: A neurologist's quest for what makes us human.* New York: Norton.

Rizzolatti, G., & Sinigaglia, C. (2008). *Mirrors in the brain: How our minds share actions and emotions.* New York: Oxford University Press.

Rock, D. (2009). *Your brain at work.* New York: Harpers.

Rupp, L., & Coleman-Lochner, L. (2014, May). "Golf stuck in a bunker as thousands leave the sport." Retrieved from https://www.bloomberg.com/news/articles/2014-05-23/golf-market-stuck-in-bunker-as-thousands-leave-the-sport.

Saplakogulu, Y. (2019, Nov). "How the brain still works when half of it is missing." Retrieved from https://www.livescience.com/hemisphere-removed-brain-plasticity.html.

Schmidt, R., Strable, U., & Schlopp, S. (2013, Feb.). "Neurogenesis in zebra fish: From embryo to adult." *Neural Development. 8*(3).

Seligman, M. (1991). *Learned optimism: How to change your mind and your life.* New York: Knopf.

Shah, S., Horne, A., & Capellá, J. (2012, Apr.) "Good data won't guarantee good decisions." *Harvard Business Review.* Retrieved from https://hbr.org/2012/04/good-data-wont-guarantee-good-decisions.

Shen, J. (2013, May). "The science of practice: What happens when you learn a new skill?" *Psychology.* Retrieved from https://lifehacker.com/the-science-of-what-happens-when-you-learn-a-510255025.

Shoemaker, F. (1997). *Extraordinary golf: The art of the possible.* New York: Penguin.

Siff, M. (2003). *Supertraining.* Denver: Supertraining Institute.

Snead, S. (1996). *Better golf the Sam Snead way.* New York: Contemporary.

Srangl, D., & Thuret, S. (2009, Aug.). "Impact of diet on adult hippocampal neurogenesis." *Genes Nutrition. 4*(4), 271–282.

Suen, W. (2004, April). "The self-perpetuation of biased beliefs." *Economic Journal. 114* (495), 377–396.

Suzuki, W. (2015). *Healthy brain, happy life.* New York: Harper Collins.

Sweet, V. (2018). *Slow Medicine: The Way to Healing.* New York: Penguin Books.

Taylor, J., & Estanol, E. (2015). *Dance psychology for artistic and performance excellence.* Champaign, Il: Human Kinetics.

Toffler, A. (1971). *Future Shock.* New York: Bantam Books.

Tolman, E.C. (1948). "Cognitive maps in rats and men." *Psychological Review.* 55(4). 189–208.

Topol, E. (2019, March 2). "The A.I. diet." *New York Times.* Retrieved from https://www.nytimes.com/2019/03/02/opinion/sunday/diet-artificial -intelligence-diabetes.html.

Toski, B., & Battersby, G. (2016, Sept. 22). "What Bob Toski tells young players." *Golf Digest.* Retrieved from: https://golfdigest.com/story /what-bob-toski-tells-young-players.

Tversky, A.N. (2003). *Preference, belief, and similarity: Selected writings.* Denver: Bradford.

Vine, S., Moore, L., & Wilson, M. (2011, Jan.). "Quiet eye training facilitates competitive putting performance." *Frontiers in Psychology.* 2(8).

Wolfram, S. (2002). *A new kind of science.* Champaign, IL: Wolfram Media.

Wulf, G. (2007). *Attention and motor skill learning.* Champaign, IL: Kinetics.

Wulf, G. & Su, J. (2007): "An external focus of attention enhances golf shot accuracy in beginners and experts." *Research Quarterly for Exercise and Sport.* 78(4) 384–389.

Zapletal, K. (2017, Mar.). "The magic of neurogenesis: How to help your body make new brain cells." *Observer.* Retrieved from http://observer .com/2017/03/the-magia-of-neurogenesis-help-your-body-brain-cells -development-entrepreneurship-health-neuroscience/.